Betty Crocker's

NEW ITALIAN
COOKING

MACMILLAN • USA

MACMILLAN
A Prentice Hall Macmillan Company
15 Columbus Circle
New York, New York 10023

MACMILLAN is a registered trademark of Macmillan, Inc.
BETTY CROCKER and BISQUICK are registered trademarks of General Mills, Inc.

Library of Congress Cataloging-in-Publication Data
Crocker, Betty.
    [New Italian cooking]
    Betty Crocker's new Italian cooking.
      p.   cm.
    Revision of: Betty Crocker's Italian cooking. New York: Prentice Hall Press, 1991.
    Includes index.
    ISBN 0-02-860031-2
    1. Cookery, Italian.   I. Crocker, Betty. Betty Crocker's Italian cooking. II. Title. III. Title:
New Italian cooking.
  TX723.C698 1995
  641.5945—dc20   94-24256
                   CIP
GENERAL MILLS, INC.
Betty Crocker Food and Publications Center
Director: Marcia Copeland
Editor: Lori Fox
Recipe Development: Antonio Cecconi
Food Stylists: Kate Courtney Condon and Cindy Lund
Nutrition Department
Nutritionists: Elyse Cohen and Nancy Holmes
Photographic Services
Photographer: Nanci Doonan Dixon

Manufactured in the United States of America

10 9 8 7 6 5 4 3 2 1

First Edition
Cover: Fresh Tomato Sauce and Noodles (page 84)
Back cover: Cannoli (page 160)

Contents

Introduction

We love Italian Food! Pasta, pizza and antipasto appetizers have been staples for years, and now we've come to appreciate other Italian treats, such as creamy risotto, fresh-from-the-skillet frittatas and crunchy biscotti or Tira Mi Su for dessert.

We think that this book presents the very best of Italian cooking, from tried-and-true favorites to adventurous new dining ideas. You'll find an entire chapter on pizza and bread, with great new pizza ideas, easy breadsticks and flavorful foccacias.

There's also a whole chapter on pasta and sauces! You can learn how to make you own pasta, or enjoy these delicious recipes with purchased pasta. Savor old favorites such as Spaghetti and Meatballs and Manicotti, then try Fettuccine alla "Bravo!" or Vermicelli with Fresh Herbs for new dinner ideas.

You'll enjoy the chapter on appetizers and soups, from Bruschetta Romana to hearty Minestrone. And we have terrific main dish recipes for chicken, seafood and meat. You're sure to appreciate Chicken Marengo, Steamed Mussels in Wine Sauce and Veal Parmesan. Looking for some snappy side dishes? You'll appreciate Neapolitan Potatoes, Baked Fennel or Caesar Salad, all with an Italian flair.

Expand your repertoire with a risotto, polenta or frittata main dish—you'll be delighted. Then, there's dessert! Sample Cannoli, Lemon Ice, or a delicious Tira Mi Su. With so many wonderful recipes, you can eat Italian anytime.

We have also included easy-to-use identification photographs of pasta, Italian cheeses, oils and vinegars, and Italian beverages. You'll be a pro in no time!

So, whether you are new to the delights of Italian cooking, or want to learn more about Italian cuisine, we think you'll find this delicious collection of recipes to be a terrific guide.

THE BETTY CROCKER EDITORS

5

1

Antipasto and Soup

Bruschetta Romana (page 11); Basil Rice Soup (page 20)

Mixed Antipasto Platter

Marinated mushrooms and artichoke hearts are packaged in glass jars and can be found shelved with the olives and pickles in the supermarket.

> *2 cloves garlic*
> *24 slices hard-crusted Italian or French bread, each 1/2-inch thick*
> *12 slices (1/2 ounce each) prosciutto or fully cooked, thinly sliced Virginia ham, cut in half*
> *12 slices (1 ounce each) provolone cheese, cut in half*
> *24 thin slices (1/2 ounce each) Genoa salami*
> *24 marinated mushrooms*
> *24 marinated artichoke hearts*
> *24 imported Kalamata or ripe olives, pitted*
> *1/2 cup extra-virgin olive or vegetable oil*
> *2 tablespoons lemon juice*
> *1 tablespoon chopped fresh or 1 teaspoon dried oregano leaves*

Cut each garlic clove in half; rub cut sides over both sides of bread. Arrange bread in single layer on serving platter. Top each bread slice with prosciutto, cheese, salami, mushroom, artichoke heart and olive. Drizzle with oil. Squeeze lemon juice over top. Sprinkle with oregano. *24 servings.*

Nutrition Information Per Serving

1 serving		Percent of U.S. RDA	
Calories	255	Vitamin A	4%
Protein, g	11	Vitamin C	6%
Carbohydrate, g	15	Calcium	14%
Fat, g	17	Iron	8%
Cholesterol, mg	30		
Sodium, mg	780		

Spicy Meatballs

Like a bit more "heat"? Use the jalapeño chili seeds instead of discarding them.

> *1 pound extra-lean ground beef*
> *1 tablespoon grated Parmesan cheese*
> *1 teaspoon dried oregano leaves*
> *1/2 teaspoon dried basil leaves*
> *1/2 teaspoon garlic salt*
> *1/2 teaspoon pepper*
> *1 egg*
> *2 tablespoons lemon juice*
> *1/4 cup olive or vegetable oil*
> *1 clove garlic, finely chopped*
> *1 small red jalapeño chili, seeded and finely chopped*
> *1 small red onion, finely chopped (about 1/4 cup)*
> *4 medium tomatoes, chopped (about 3 cups)*
> *1 tablespoon dry red wine or chicken broth*

Mix ground beef, cheese, oregano, basil, garlic salt, pepper, egg and lemon juice. Shape mixture into 1-inch balls.

Heat oil in 10-inch skillet over medium-high heat. Cook garlic, chili and onion in oil 5 to 7 minutes, stirring frequently, until onion is crisp-tender. Add meatballs. Cook, turning meatballs, until meatballs are brown. Stir in tomatoes and wine; reduce heat. Cover and simmer 30 minutes, stirring occasionally. Serve in chafing dish if desired. *6 servings.*

Nutrition Information Per Serving

1 serving		Percent of U.S. RDA	
Calories	280	Vitamin A	14%
Protein, g	15	Vitamin C	30%
Carbohydrate, g	7	Calcium	4%
Fat, g	22	Iron	12%
Cholesterol, mg	80		
Sodium, mg	160		

Mixed Antipasto Platter

Caponata

Kalamata olives, known as the "Cadillac" of olives, are imported from Greece. The plump, purplish to black olives have a moist texture and a robust, wine-like flavor.

2 large eggplant
1 tablespoon salt
3 tablespoons olive or vegetable oil
18 imported Kalamata olives or ripe olives, pitted
4 medium tomatoes, chopped (about 3 cups)
2 cloves garlic, finely chopped
1 tablespoon capers
1 tablespoon pine nuts
2 tablespoons wine vinegar
2 teaspoons sugar
1/2 teaspoon pepper

Peel eggplant; cut into 1/2-inch cubes. Spread eggplant on cutting board; sprinkle with salt. Tilt board slightly; let stand 30 minutes. Rinse eggplant; pat dry.

Heat oil in 12-inch nonstick skillet over medium-high heat. Add remaining ingredients. Cook uncovered over medium heat 20 minutes, stirring frequently until eggplant is tender. Serve warm or cold. *6 servings.*

Nutrition Information Per Serving

1 serving		Percent of U.S. RDA	
Calories	180	Vitamin A	12%
Protein, g	3	Vitamin C	28%
Carbohydrate, g	25	Calcium	4%
Fat, g	10	Iron	10%
Cholesterol, mg	0		
Sodium, mg	1190		

Antipasto

Antipasto literally means "before the pasta" and is served as an appetizer. In Italy almost all antipasto dishes are prepared in advance and served at room temperature, although a few are served warm. Antipasto tempts the diner visually as well as with its taste, and a colorful antipasto reflects the creativity of the cook as well as stimulates the appetite.

Antipasto has three basic types. *Freddi e crudi* includes raw vegetables and cold meats, fish and cheese. These can be served by themselves or in various combinations. *Affettati* includes cured meats sliced just before serving and accompanied by crusty breads or breadsticks. Prosciutto is the most popular example and is served by itself or with fresh cantaloupe or fresh figs. *Antipasto caldi* are fried or baked morsels, just large enough to take the edge off a diner's hunger without being too filling. They range from batter fritters such as fried zucchini blossoms to baked mussels and seasoned bread tarts such as bruschetta and crostini.

Basil Toast

Freshly ground black pepper adds the perfect touch to these tasty appetizers.

1 large tomato, chopped (about 1 cup)
3 tablespoons chopped fresh basil leaves
1 tablespoon capers
1/2 teaspoon salt
1/2 teaspoon pepper
12 slices Italian or French bread, each
  1/2 inch thick
1/4 cup olive or vegetable oil
12 slices (1 ounce each) mozzarella cheese

Heat oven to 375°. Mix tomato, basil, capers, salt and pepper. Place bread on ungreased cookie sheet. Drizzle 1 teaspoon oil on each slice of bread. Spoon half the tomato mixture onto bread. Top each with cheese slice. Spoon remaining tomato mixture onto cheese. Bake about 8 minutes or until hot and cheese is melted. *6 servings.*

Nutrition Information Per Serving

1 serving		Percent of U.S. RDA	
Calories	310	Vitamin A	8%
Protein, g	15	Vitamin C	4%
Carbohydrate, g	25	Calcium	10%
Fat, g	17	Iron	34%
Cholesterol, mg	25		
Sodium, mg	640		

Bruschetta Romana

1 jar (7 ounces) roasted red bell peppers,
  drained and cut into 1/2-inch strips
1 to 2 medium cloves garlic, finely
  chopped
2 tablespoons chopped fresh parsley or
  1 teaspoon dried parsley flakes
2 tablespoons freshly shredded Parmesan
  cheese
1 tablespoon olive or vegetable oil
1/4 teaspoon salt
1/4 teaspoon pepper
8 slices hard-crusted Italian or French
  bread, each 1/2 inch thick

Heat oven to 450°. Mix all ingredients except bread. Place bread on ungreased cookie sheet. Spoon pepper mixture onto bread. Bake 6 to 8 minutes or until edges of bread are golden brown. *4 servings.*

Nutrition Information Per Serving

1 serving		Percent of U.S. RDA	
Calories	160	Vitamin A	12%
Protein, g	5	Vitamin C	42%
Carbohydrate, g	25	Calcium	8%
Fat, g	5	Iron	8%
Cholesterol, mg	5		
Sodium, mg	430		

Olive Cream Cheese Spread

For truly authentic Italian flavor, substitute mascarpone cheese for the cream cheese.

*1 package (8 ounces) cream cheese,
    softened*
¹/₄ cup grated Parmesan cheese
1 tablespoon sliced pimiento-stuffed olives
1 tablespoon sliced ripe olives
*2 teaspoons chopped fresh or ¹/₂ teaspoon
    freeze-dried chives*
¹/₄ teaspoon pepper
¹/₂ cup slivered almonds, toasted
*1 tablespoon chopped fresh or 1 teaspoon
    dried basil leaves*

Mix all ingredients except almonds and basil. Cover and refrigerate 1 hour. Just before serving, sprinkle with almonds and basil. Serve with crackers and bread if desired. *About 2 cups spread.*

Nutrition Information Per Serving

1 tablespoon		Percent of U.S. RDA	
Calories	170	Vitamin A	8%
Protein, g	5	Vitamin C	*
Carbohydrate, g	3	Calcium	8%
Fat, g	16	Iron	4%
Cholesterol, mg	35		
Sodium, mg	230		

Herbed Zucchini Slices

Salting and draining the zucchini draws out excess moisture, which allows the slices to retain more of their texture during cooking.

*2 medium zucchini, cut lengthwise into
    ¹/₄-inch slices*
¹/₄ teaspoon salt
*1 tablespoon chopped fresh or 1 teaspoon
    dried basil leaves*
*1 tablespoon chopped fresh parsley or
    1 teaspoon dried parsley flakes*
1 tablespoon olive or vegetable oil
¹/₄ teaspoon salt
¹/₈ teaspoon pepper
2 green onions, finely chopped
1 clove garlic, finely chopped

Heat oven to 450°. Line broiler pan with aluminum foil. Place zucchini on cutting board; sprinkle with ¹/₄ teaspoon salt. Tilt board slightly; let stand 15 minutes. Rinse and drain zucchini; pat dry with paper towels. Cut zucchini slices crosswise in half. Place zucchini in pan.

Mix remaining ingredients. Sprinkle over zucchini. Bake 4 to 8 minutes or until zucchini is crisp-tender. *4 servings.*

Nutrition Information Per Serving

1 serving		Percent of U.S. RDA	
Calories	50	Vitamin A	4%
Protein, g	1	Vitamin C	10%
Carbohydrate, g	4	Calcium	2%
Fat, g	4	Iron	4%
Cholesterol, mg	0		
Sodium, mg	270		

Olive Cream Cheese Spread; Herbed Zucchini Slices

Calamari

Calamari, or squid, is an Italian delicacy. If you can't find squid at the supermarket, it should be available at a fish market.

Vegetable oil
1 pound cleaned fresh squid tail cones
    (calamari)
1 egg, slightly beaten
1 tablespoon lemon juice
1/2 cup all-purpose flour
1 cup seasoned dry bread crumbs
Salt and pepper to taste
1 lemon, sliced
Fresh parsley, if desired

Heat oil (2 inches) in deep fryer or Dutch oven to 375°. Wash squid; pat dry. Cut squid into 1/4-inch slices. Mix egg and lemon juice in small bowl. Coat squid with flour; shake off excess flour. Dip squid into egg mixture; coat with bread crumbs.

Fry about 1 minute or until golden brown; drain on paper towels. Sprinkle with salt and pepper. Garnish with lemon slices and, if desired, fresh parsley sprigs. *6 servings.*

Nutrition Information Per Serving

1 serving		Percent of U.S. RDA	
Calories	215	Vitamin A	2%
Protein, g	14	Vitamin C	2%
Carbohydrate, g	15	Calcium	2%
Fat, g	11	Iron	6%
Cholesterol, mg	180		
Sodium, mg	570		

Steamed Mussels in Wine Sauce

24 fresh large mussels (about 2 pounds)
1 tablespoon olive or vegetable oil
1/2 cup chopped fresh parsley
2 cloves garlic, finely chopped
1 cup dry white wine or chicken broth
1/2 teaspoon salt
1/4 teaspoon pepper

Discard any broken shells or open (dead) mussels. Wash remaining mussels, removing any barnacles with a dull paring knife. Remove beards by tugging thcm away from shells.

Heat oil in 12-inch skillet over medium-high heat. Cook parsley and garlic in oil, stirring frequently, until garlic is soft. Add mussels, wine, salt and pepper. Cover and cook 10 minutes or until shells open. (Discard any mussels if shells do not open.) Drizzle liquid from skillet over each serving. *4 servings.*

Nutrition Information Per Serving

1 serving		Percent of U.S. RDA	
Calories	130	Vitamin A	12%
Protein, g	16	Vitamin C	10%
Carbohydrate, g	5	Calcium	6%
Fat, g	5	Iron	98%
Cholesterol, mg	40		
Sodium, mg	340		

Savory Mushrooms

If you have access to portobello mushrooms, they are perfect in this dish! Portobello mushrooms, common in Italian cooking, are large and white with a meaty texture.

8 large mushrooms
2 green onions, finely chopped
2 cloves garlic, finely chopped
1 tablespoon chopped fresh parsley or
    1 teaspoon dried parsley flakes
2 tablespoons olive or vegetable oil
1/2 teaspoon salt
1/2 teaspoon pepper

Heat oven to 450°. Remove stems from mushrooms; finely chop stems. Mix stems, onions, garlic and parsley in small bowl. Stir in oil, salt and pepper.

Fill mushroom caps with stem mixture. Place mushrooms, filled sides up, in an ungreased square baking dish, 8 × 8 × 2 inches. Bake 15 to 20 minutes or until mushrooms are tender. Spoon drippings in baking dish over mushrooms before serving. *4 servings.*

Nutrition Information Per Serving

1 serving		Percent of U.S. RDA	
Calories	75	Vitamin A	*
Protein, g	1	Vitamin C	4%
Carbohydrate, g	3	Calcium	*
Fat, g	7	Iron	4%
Cholesterol, mg	0		
Sodium, mg	270		

Vegetable Minestrone

2 tablespoons olive or vegetable oil
2 cloves garlic, finely chopped
1 medium onion, coarsely chopped (about
    1/2 cup)
3 cans (14 1/2 ounces each) vegetable broth
1 package (10 ounces) frozen lima beans,
    thawed
2 medium carrots, sliced (about 1 cup)
1 medium potato, peeled and cubed (about
    1 cup)
1 small tomato, diced (about 1/2 cup)
1/2 cup finely chopped red or green
    cabbage
1 tablespoon chopped fresh parsley or
    1 teaspoon dried parsley flakes
1 tablespoon chopped fresh or 1 teaspoon
    dried basil leaves
2 teaspoons chopped fresh or 1/4 teaspoon
    dried dill weed
1 bay leaf
1/2 cup uncooked farfalle (bow-tie) pasta or
    small pasta shells

Heat oil in 3-quart saucepan over medium-high heat. Cook garlic and onion in oil 1 minute, stirring frequently. Stir in remaining ingredients except pasta. Heat to boiling; reduce heat. Cover and simmer 15 minutes. Stir in pasta. Cover and simmer 10 to 15 minutes or until pasta is tender. Remove bay leaf. *6 servings.*

Nutrition Information Per Serving

1 serving		Percent of U.S. RDA	
Calories	200	Vitamin A	56%
Protein, g	10	Vitamin C	14%
Carbohydrate, g	29	Calcium	4%
Fat, g	5	Iron	10%
Cholesterol, mg	0		
Sodium, mg	590		

Minestrone

2 beef shanks (about 1 pound)
1 tablespoon olive or vegetable oil
1 clove garlic, finely chopped
2 tablespoons chopped onion
2 large romaine leaves, torn into bite-size
pieces
2 large red cabbage leaves, coarsely
chopped
1 medium potato, chopped (about 1 cup)
1 medium carrot, chopped (about ¹/₂ cup)
4 quarts water
¹/₂ cup dried split peas
1 tablespoon salt
¹/₂ teaspoon pepper
2 medium stalks celery, chopped (about
1 cup)
1 medium tomato, chopped (about
³/₄ cup)
1 bay leaf
1 cup uncooked rotini pasta

Remove bones and fat from beef shanks; cut beef into 1-inch pieces. Heat oil in 6-quart Dutch oven over medium-high heat. Cook beef, garlic and onion in oil, stirring occasionally, until beef is light brown.

Stir in romaine, cabbage, potato and carrot. Cook uncovered about 5 minutes, stirring frequently, until romaine is wilted.

Stir in remaining ingredients except pasta. Heat to boiling; reduce heat. Cover and simmer 40 minutes. Stir in pasta. Cover and simmer about 10 minutes or until pasta is tender. Remove bay leaf. *8 servings.*

Nutrition Information Per Serving

1 serving		Percent of U.S. RDA	
Calories	170	Vitamin A	16%
Protein, g	13	Vitamin C	8%
Carbohydrate, g	26	Calcium	2%
Fat, g	3	Iron	10%
Cholesterol, mg	20		
Sodium, mg	830		

Minestrone

Fresh Mint Soup

2 tablespoons olive or vegetable oil
1 large onion, chopped (about 1 cup)
6 slices bacon, chopped
3 medium tomatoes, chopped (about 2¹/₄ cups)
2 medium zucchini, chopped (about 4 cups)
1 large potato, shredded (about 2 cups)
1 cup chicken broth
1 cup water
³/₄ cup chopped fresh mint leaves
1 teaspoon salt
¹/₂ teaspoon pepper
¹/₄ cup chopped fresh mint leaves

Heat oil in 3-quart saucepan over medium-low heat. Cover and cook onion in oil 10 minutes, stirring occasionally. Stir in bacon. Cook uncovered over medium heat about 10 minutes, stirring occasionally, until bacon is translucent.

Stir in tomatoes, zucchini and potato. Cover and cook over medium-low heat 10 minutes. Stir in remaining ingredients except ¹/₄ cup mint. Heat to boiling; reduce heat. Cover and simmer 1 hour, stirring occasionally. Top each serving with mint. *6 servings.*

Nutrition Information Per Serving

1 serving		Percent of U.S. RDA	
Calories	140	Vitamin A	8%
Protein, g	5	Vitamin C	26%
Carbohydrate, g	15	Calcium	2%
Fat, g	8	Iron	6%
Cholesterol, mg	5		
Sodium, mg	600		

Soups

Italian cooking has three types of soups. Although they all begin with a meat, seafood or vegetable broth, their final flavors, appearance and textures are quite different. *Zuppe* are the heartiest soups, in which vegetables and meat form a dense, chunky mixture. An excellent example of a zuppa is Minestrone (page 16)—which is almost a complete meal in itself. *Minestre* start with a light broth to which pasta, a vegetable or sometimes seafood is added to give depth and subtle flavor. This lighter soup, such as Basil Rice Soup (page 20) is an ideal first course, a prelude to a heartier *secondo*, or entrée. *Creme* are smooth, creamy soups made with milk and/or cream.

Onion and Potato Soup

3 tablespoons margarine or butter
2 large white onions, thinly sliced
2 tablespoons chopped fresh parsley
2 cloves garlic, finely chopped
2 bay leaves
1/2 cup diced prosciutto or fully cooked
    Virginia ham (about 4 ounces)
4 cups chicken broth
3 cups water
1 teaspoon pepper
4 large potatoes, shredded (about 4 cups)
1/4 cup freshly grated Romano cheese

Melt margarine in Dutch oven over medium-low heat. Cover and cook onions in margarine 10 minutes, stirring occasionally. Stir in parsley, garlic, bay leaves and prosciutto. Cook uncovered over high heat 5 minutes, stirring frequently.

Stir in remaining ingredients except cheese. Heat to boiling; reduce heat. Cover and simmer 30 minutes, stirring occasionally. Remove bay leaves. Top each serving with cheese. *4 servings.*

Nutrition Information Per Serving

1 serving		Percent of U.S. RDA	
Calories	330	Vitamin A	8%
Protein, g	14	Vitamin C	22%
Carbohydrate, g	39	Calcium	8%
Fat, g	15	Iron	10%
Cholesterol, mg	40		
Sodium, mg	1070		

Chunky Tomato Soup

2 tablespoons olive or vegetable oil
2 cloves garlic, chopped
2 medium stalks celery, coarsely chopped
    (about 1 cup)
2 medium carrots, coarsely chopped
    (about 1 cup)
2 cans (28 ounces each) whole Italian-
    style tomatoes, undrained
4 cups water
3 1/2 cups chicken broth
1 teaspoon dried basil leaves
1/2 teaspoon pepper
2 bay leaves
8 slices hard-crusted Italian or French
    bread, each 1 inch thick, toasted

Heat oil in Dutch oven over medium-high heat. Cook garlic, celery and carrots in oil for 5 to 7 minutes, stirring frequently, until carrots are crisp-tender. Stir in tomatoes; break up tomatoes coarsely. Stir in remaining ingredients except bread. Heat to boiling; reduce heat. Cover and simmer 1 hour, stirring occasionally. Remove bay leaves.

Place 1 slice toast in each of 8 bowls. Ladle soup over toast. Serve immediately. *8 servings.*

Nutrition Information Per Serving

1 serving		Percent of U.S. RDA	
Calories	170	Vitamin A	40%
Protein, g	7	Vitamin C	26%
Carbohydrate, g	28	Calcium	10%
Fat, g	5	Iron	14%
Cholesterol, mg	0		
Sodium, mg	840		

Basil Rice Soup

2 tablespoons olive or vegetable oil
2 cloves garlic, finely chopped
2 medium stalks celery, chopped (about 1 cup)
1 medium onion, chopped (about 1/2 cup)
1 medium carrot, chopped (about 1/2 cup)
1/4 cup chopped fresh basil leaves
3/4 cup uncooked regular long grain rice
2 medium tomatoes, chopped (about 1 1/2 cups)
4 cups chicken broth
1 cup water
1 teaspoon salt
1/4 teaspoon pepper
1/4 cup grated Romano cheese

Heat oil in Dutch oven over medium-low heat. Cover and cook garlic, celery, onion, carrot and basil in oil 10 minutes, stirring occasionally. Stir in rice and tomatoes. Cook uncovered over medium heat 5 minutes, stirring occasionally.

Stir in remaining ingredients except cheese. Heat to boiling; reduce heat. Cover and simmer about 20 minutes or until rice is tender. Top each serving with cheese. *6 servings.*

Nutrition Information Per Serving

1 serving		Percent of U.S. RDA	
Calories	190	Vitamin A	24%
Protein, g	7	Vitamin C	12%
Carbohydrate, g	27	Calcium	6%
Fat, g	7	Iron	10%
Cholesterol, mg	5		
Sodium, mg	940		

Tortellini Soup

For a pretty color contrast, try using half spinach and half plain tortellini.

3 tablespoons margarine or butter
2 cloves garlic, finely chopped
2 medium stalks celery, chopped (about 1 cup)
1 medium carrot, chopped (about 1/2 cup)
1 small onion, chopped (about 1/4 cup)
8 cups chicken broth
4 cups water
2 packages (9 ounces each) dried cheese-filled tortellini
2 tablespoons chopped fresh parsley
1/2 teaspoon pepper
1 teaspoon freshly grated nutmeg
Freshly grated Parmesan cheese, if desired

Melt margarine in 6-quart Dutch oven over medium-low heat. Cover and cook garlic, celery, carrot and onion in margarine 10 minutes, stirring occasionally. Stir in broth and water. Heat to boiling; reduce heat. Stir in tortellini. Cover and simmer about 20 minutes, stirring occasionally, until tortellini are tender. Stir in parsley, pepper and nutmeg. Cover and simmer 10 minutes. Top each serving with cheese. *8 servings.*

Nutrition Information Per Serving

1 serving		Percent of U.S. RDA	
Calories	375	Vitamin A	18%
Protein, g	17	Vitamin C	2%
Carbohydrate, g	59	Calcium	12%
Fat, g	9	Iron	20%
Cholesterol, mg	15		
Sodium, mg	940		

Tortellini Soup

Spinach Polenta Soup

The addition of yellow cornmeal helps to thicken this hearty soup to just the right consistency.

2 tablespoons olive or vegetable oil
2 cloves garlic, finely chopped
1 medium onion, finely chopped (about
    1/2 cup)
1 package (16 ounces) frozen cut leaf or
    chopped spinach
3 cans (141/2 ounces each) vegetable broth
1/2 cup yellow cornmeal
1 tablespoon grated Parmesan cheese
1 tablespoon chopped fresh parsley or
    1 teaspoon dried parsley flakes
1/4 teaspoon ground nutmeg
1/4 teaspoon pepper

Heat oil in 3-quart saucepan over medium heat. Cook garlic and onion in oil 5 minutes, stirring occasionally, until crisp-tender. Stir in frozen spinach and broth. Heat to boiling; reduce heat. Stir in remaining ingredients. Cover and simmer about 15 minutes, stirring frequently, until soup is slightly thickened. *8 servings.*

Nutrition Information Per Serving

1 serving		Percent of U.S. RDA	
Calories	345	Vitamin A	100%
Protein, g	31	Vitamin C	66%
Carbohydrate, g	50	Calcium	92%
Fat, g	8	Iron	60%
Cholesterol, mg	30		
Sodium, mg	880		

Lentil Soup

You can use either brown or green lentils in this robust soup.

2 tablespoons olive or vegetable oil
2 cloves garlic, finely chopped
1 medium onion, finely chopped (about
    1/2 cup)
1 bay leaf
1/2 cup diced prosciutto or fully cooked
    Virginia ham (about 4 ounces)
1/4 cup diced Genoa salami (about 2
    ounces)
4 cups water
2 cups chicken broth
11/2 cups dried lentils (about 8 ounces),
    sorted and rinsed
1/2 teaspoon pepper
shredded carrot, if desired

Heat oil in Dutch oven over medium-high heat. Cook garlic, onion and bay leaf in oil 5 to 7 minutes, stirring frequently, until onion is tender. Stir in prosciutto and salami. Cook uncovered over medium heat 10 minutes, stirring frequently. Stir in remaining ingredients. Heat to boiling; reduce heat. Cover and simmer 1 hour, stirring occasionally. Remove bay leaf. Sprinkle servings with shredded carrot. *4 servings.*

Nutrition Information Per Serving

1 serving		Percent of U.S. RDA	
Calories	370	Vitamin A	*
Protein, g	27	Vitamin C	8%
Carbohydrate, g	46	Calcium	6%
Fat, g	14	Iron	42%
Cholesterol, mg	20		
Sodium, mg	1260		

Chicken Noodle Soup

Ground nutmeg adds a delightful new twist to a traditional favorite.

2 tablespoons olive or vegetable oil
2 cloves garlic, finely chopped
2 green onions, chopped
1 medium carrot, chopped (about ½ cup)
5½ cups chicken broth
2 cups cubed cooked chicken
1 cup 2-inch pieces uncooked spaghetti
1 tablespoon chopped fresh parsley or
    1 teaspoon dried parsley flakes
½ teaspoon ground nutmeg
¼ teaspoon pepper
1 bay leaf

Heat oil in 3-quart saucepan over medium heat. Cook garlic, onions and carrot in oil 4 minutes, stirring occasionally. Stir in remaining ingredients. Heat to boiling; reduce heat. Cover and simmer about 15 minutes, stirring occasionally, until carrot and spaghetti are tender. *4 servings.*

Nutrition Information Per Serving

1 serving		Percent of U.S. RDA	
Calories	275	Vitamin A	28%
Protein, g	28	Vitamin C	4%
Carbohydrate, g	12	Calcium	4%
Fat, g	13	Iron	14%
Cholesterol, mg	60		
Sodium, mg	1040		

2

Pizza and Bread

Mediterranean Peppered Pizza (page 45)

White Bread

4 packages active dry yeast
1 cup warm water (105° to 115°)
1 cup warm milk (105° to 115°)
5¹/₂ to 6 cups bread flour or all-purpose
*   flour*
1 tablespoon salt
1 tablespoon margarine or butter, softened
1 teaspoon sugar

Dissolve yeast in warm water in large bowl. Stir in milk, 4 cups of the flour, the salt, margarine and sugar. Stir in enough of the remaining flour to make dough easy to handle. Turn dough onto lightly floured surface. Knead 5 minutes. Cover and let rest 20 minutes.

Knead dough on lightly floured surface about 10 minutes or until smooth and elastic. Place in greased bowl, turning to coat all sides. Cover and let rise in warm place about 45 minutes or until double. (Dough is ready if indentation remains when touched.)

Grease cookie sheet. Punch down dough. Roll into rectangle, 14 × 10 inches, on lightly floured surface. Roll up tightly, beginning at 10-inch side. Pinch edge of dough into roll to seal well. Roll gently back and forth to taper ends. Place seam side down on cookie sheet. Cover and let rise in warm place about 30 minutes or until double.

Heat oven to 325°. Make 3 slashes, about ¹/₄ inch deep, across loaf; dust with flour. Bake about 55 minutes or until loaf is golden brown and sounds hollow when tapped. Remove from cookie sheet. Cool on wire rack. *1 loaf (16 slices).*

Nutrition Information Per Serving

1 slice		Percent of U.S. RDA	
Calories	195	Vitamin A	*
Protein, g	6	Vitamin C	*
Carbohydrate, g	38	Calcium	2%
Fat, g	2	Iron	14%
Cholesterol, mg	5		
Sodium, mg	410		

Easy Onion and Herb Focaccia

Try serving wedges of this fresh focaccia with Olive Cream Cheese Spread (page 12)—delicious!

1 can (10 ounces) refrigerated pizza
*   dough*
1 tablespoon olive or vegetable oil
1 tablespoon finely chopped red onion
2 teaspoons chopped fresh or 1 teaspoon
*   dried sage leaves*
2 teaspoons chopped fresh or ¹/₂ teaspoon
*   dried rosemary leaves*

Heat oven to 425°. Grease cookie sheet or 12-inch pizza pan. Unroll dough; place on cookie sheet. Press dough from center to edge into 12-inch circle. Brush with oil. Sprinkle with remaining ingredients. Bake 10 to 12 minutes or until golden brown. *12 servings.*

Nutrition Information Per Serving

1 serving		Percent of U.S. RDA	
Calories	90	Vitamin A	*
Protein, g	2	Vitamin C	*
Carbohydrate, g	14	Calcium	*
Fat, g	3	Iron	4%
Cholesterol, mg	0		
Sodium, mg	120		

Easy Onion and Herb Focaccia

Italian Flatbread

Italian flatbread, or focaccia, is becoming more and more popular, so we've given you four delicious toppings to suit your various meals and moods!

1 package active dry yeast
1 cup warm water (105° to 115°)
¼ cup olive or vegetable oil
2 teaspoons sugar
¼ teaspoon salt
2½ to 3 cups all-purpose flour
Vegetable oil
Basil Topping, Parmesan Topping, Red
*   Pepper Topping or Salt Topping*
*   (right), if desired*

Dissolve yeast in warm water in large bowl. Add ¼ cup oil, the sugar, salt and 2 cups of the flour. Beat on medium speed 3 minutes, scraping bowl occasionally. Stir in enough of the remaining flour until dough is soft and leaves side of bowl.

Turn dough onto lightly floured surface. Knead 5 to 10 minutes or until dough is smooth and elastic. Place in greased bowl, turning to coat all sides. Cover and let rise in warm place 1 to 1½ hours or until double.

Grease 2 cookie sheets. Punch down dough; divide in half. Press each half into 12-inch circle on cookie sheet. Cover and let rise in warm place 20 minutes.

Heat oven to 425°. Prick rims of circles 1 inch from edge with fork. Prick centers of circles thoroughly with fork. Brush circles with vegetable oil. Add topping below, if desired. Bake 12 to 15 minutes or until golden brown. *2 flatbreads (12 servings each).*

BASIL TOPPING: Sprinkle each flatbread with 1 tablespoon chopped fresh basil leaves or other fresh herb.

PARMESAN TOPPING: Sprinkle each flatbread with 1 tablespoon grated Parmesan cheese.

RED PEPPER TOPPING: Cook 2 medium red bell peppers, cut into ¼-inch rings, and 1 medium onion, sliced, in 1 tablespoon olive or vegetable oil in 10-inch skillet, stirring occasionally, just until tender. Arrange on flatbreads.

SALT TOPPING: Sprinkle each flatbread with ½ to ¾ teaspoon coarse (kosher) salt.

Nutrition Information Per Serving

1 serving		Percent of U.S. RDA	
Calories	60	Vitamin A	*
Protein, g	1	Vitamin C	*
Carbohydrate, g	10	Calcium	*
Fat, g	2	Iron	4%
Cholesterol, mg	0		
Sodium, mg	25		

Spicy Breadsticks

Basic Pizza Dough for Three Crusts
   (page 32)
1 tablespoon freshly grated Parmesan
   cheese
1 tablespoon freshly grated Romano
   cheese
1 teaspoon dried oregano leaves
1 teaspoon dried basil leaves
¹/₂ teaspoon garlic salt
¹/₂ teaspoon pepper

Prepare Basic Pizza Dough.

Heat oven to 400°. Grease 2 cookie sheets. Press or roll dough into rectangle, 24 × 12 inches, on lightly floured surface. Mix remaining ingredients; sprinkle evenly over dough. Gently press herb mixture into dough.

Cut dough into 24 strips, 12 × 1 inch. Place strips ¹/₂ inch apart on cookie sheets. Bake about 10 minutes or until golden brown. Remove from cookie sheets. Cool on wire racks. *24 breadsticks.*

Nutrition Information Per Serving

1 breadstick		Percent of U.S. RDA	
Calories	75	Vitamin A	*
Protein, g	2	Vitamin C	*
Carbohydrate, g	15	Calcium	*
Fat, g	1	Iron	6%
Cholesterol, mg	5		
Sodium, mg	120		

Quick Bread Toppers

Turn plain French or Italian bread loaves into tasty side dishes in no time!

1. Split French or Italian bread in half lengthwise or cut into individual slices; place on cookie sheet or heavy-duty aluminum foil.
2. Spread cut sides of bread halves (one side of individual slices) with margarine or butter, brush with olive oil or spray with no stick cooking spray.
3. Add one or more of the following to the cut sides (one side of individual slices) of the bread before heating.

- Spread with mixture of equal parts softened margarine or butter, mayonnaise and grated Parmesan cheese, omitting step 2 above.
- Sprinkle with fresh or dried basil or oregano leaves, finely chopped fresh onion or onion powder, fresh minced garlic or garlic powder, shredded Cheddar, mozzarella or provolone cheese.
- Sprinkle with sliced or chopped ripe or pimiento-stuffed olives. Sprinkle with freshly shredded or grated Parmesan cheese.
- Add drained canned mushrooms, chopped green onion and sprinkle with a combination of Cheddar and mozzarella cheese.
- Add chopped roasted red peppers, sun-dried tomatoes or bell peppers. Sprinkle with mozzarella or Parmesan cheese.

Italian Sweet Bread with Raisins

1 package active dry yeast
1 cup warm water (105° to 115°)
1 cup raisins
¹/₂ cup sugar
3 tablespoons vegetable oil
1 tablespoon grated orange peel
1 egg, beaten
3¹/₂ to 4 cups all-purpose flour
Milk
Sugar

Dissolve yeast in warm water in large bowl. Stir in 3 cups flour, raisins, ¹/₂ cup sugar, the oil, orange peel and egg. Stir in enough of the remaining flour to make a soft dough. Turn dough onto generously floured surface. Knead 10 to 15 minutes or until smooth and elastic. Place in greased bowl, turning to coat all sides. Cover and let rise in warm place about 1 hour or until double.

Grease cookie sheet. Punch down dough. Shape into round, 9 inches in diameter, on cookie sheet. Flatten dough slightly. Cover and let rise 45 minutes.

Heat oven to 350°. Brush loaf with milk. Sprinkle with sugar. Bake 30 to 35 minutes or until golden brown. Remove from cookie sheet. Cool on wire rack. *1 loaf (16 slices).*

Nutrition Information Per Serving

1 slice		Percent of U.S. RDA	
Calories	180	Vitamin A	*
Protein, g	3	Vitamin C	*
Carbohydrate, g	35	Calcium	*
Fat, g	3	Iron	8%
Cholesterol, mg	15		
Sodium, mg	10		

Riviera Loaf

This delicious bread is perfect with pasta and would also be a welcome appetizer!

1 loaf (8 ounces) Italian or French bread
2 tablespoons chopped ripe olives
2 tablespoons chopped pimiento-stuffed olives
2 tablespoons sun-dried tomatoes in oil, drained and chopped (reserve 1 tablespoon oil)
1 tablespoon chopped fresh parsley
2 cloves garlic, finely chopped
1 cup shredded mozzarella cheese (4 ounces)

Heat oven to 400°. Cut bread horizontally in half. Place cut sides up on ungreased cookie sheet. Mix olives, tomatoes, reserved oil, parsley and garlic; arrange over cut sides of bread. Sprinkle each half with ¹/₂ cup of the cheese. Bake 8 to 10 minutes or until cheese is melted. *6 servings.*

Nutrition Information Per Serving

1 serving		Percent of U.S. RDA	
Calories	190	Vitamin A	2%
Protein, g	9	Vitamin C	*
Carbohydrate, g	23	Calcium	18%
Fat, g	7	Iron	8%
Cholesterol, mg	10		
Sodium, mg	420		

Riviera Loaf; Lentil Soup (page 22)

Basic Pizza Dough

One Crust:

1 package active dry yeast
1/2 cup warm water (105° to 115°)
1 1/4 to 1 1/2 cups all-purpose flour
1 teaspoon olive or vegetable oil
1/2 teaspoon salt
1/4 teaspoon sugar

Two Crusts:

2 packages active dry yeast
1 cup warm water (105° to 115°)
2 1/3 to 2 2/3 cups all-purpose flour
2 teaspoons olive or vegetable oil
1 teaspoon salt
1/2 teaspoon sugar

Three Crusts:

2 packages active dry yeast
1 1/2 cups warm water (105° to 115°)
3 3/4 to 4 cups all-purpose flour
1 tablespoon olive or vegetable oil
1 teaspoon salt
1/2 teaspoon sugar

Dissolve yeast in warm water in large bowl. Stir in half of the flour, the oil, salt and sugar. Stir in enough of the remaining flour to make dough easy to handle.

Turn dough onto lightly floured surface. Knead about 10 minutes or until smooth and elastic. Place in greased bowl; turning to coat all sides. Cover and let rise in warm place 20 minutes.

Punch down dough. Use immediately or cover and refrigerate at least 2 hours but no longer than 48 hours, punching down dough as necessary.

Nutrition Information Per Serving

1 serving		Percent of U.S. RDA	
Calories	75	Vitamin A	*
Protein, g	2	Vitamin C	*
Carbohydrate, g	15	Calcium	*
Fat, g	1	Iron	6%
Cholesterol, mg	0		
Sodium, mg	135		

Sweet Bread Wreath

Basic Pizza Dough for Three Crusts
(left)
2 eggs, beaten
1/4 cup sugar
1/2 teaspoon ground cinnamon
1/2 teaspoon ground anise
1/4 teaspoon ground nutmeg

Prepare Basic Pizza Dough.

Heat oven to 350°. Grease cookie sheet. Divide dough into 3 equal parts. Roll each part dough into a rope, 26 inches long, on lightly floured surface. Braid ropes gently and loosely; pinch ends together. Shape braid into wreath on cookie sheet; pinch ends together. Cover and let rise in warm place about 1 hour or until double.

Brush wreath with eggs. Mix remaining ingredients; sprinkle on wreath. Bake 25 to 30 minutes or until golden brown. Remove from cookie sheet. Cool on wire rack. *1 wreath (16 slices).*

Nutrition Information Per Serving

1 slice		Percent of U.S. RDA	
Calories	140	Vitamin A	*
Protein, g	4	Vitamin C	*
Carbohydrate, g	26	Calcium	*
Fat, g	2	Iron	8%
Cholesterol, mg	25		
Sodium, mg	140		

Sweet Bread Wreath

Classic Pizza

Basic Pizza Dough for One Crust
(page 32)
1/2 cup Simple Pizza Sauce (page 86) or
purchased pizza sauce
1 pound bulk Italian sausage
1 small onion, chopped (about 1/4 cup)
1 cup shredded mozzarella cheese
(4 ounces)
1/2 cup shredded provolone cheese
(2 ounces)
1/4 cup chopped fresh basil leaves
1/2 cup chopped fully cooked smoked ham
or prosciutto (about 4 ounces)

Prepare Basic Pizza Dough and Simple Pizza
Sauce. Cook sausage and onion in 10-inch skillet, stirring occasionally, until sausage is brown;
drain.

Heat oven to 425°. Grease cookie sheet or
12-inch pizza pan. Press dough into 12-inch circle on cookie sheet with floured fingers. Spread
pizza sauce over dough to within 1/2 inch of
edge. Mix cheeses; sprinkle over sauce. Spread
sausage mixture over cheeses. Sprinkle with
basil and ham.

Bake 15 to 20 minutes or until crust is golden
brown and cheeses are melted. *8 servings.*

Nutrition Information Per Serving

1 serving		Percent of U.S. RDA	
Calories	740	Vitamin A	12%
Protein, g	43	Vitamin C	10%
Carbohydrate, g	38	Calcium	38%
Fat, g	46	Iron	26%
Cholesterol, mg	130		
Sodium, mg	1850		

Pizza

For Italians, pizza is an extension of
bread. Pizza in some form has always
been present throughout most of Italian
history, and every region has its favorite
variations. In a bakery shop in the ruins
of Pompeii, archaeologists found evi-
dence of a flatbread topped with
garum—a fish-and-spice paste—that
was a form of pizza. Flatbread was also
a staple for the Roman armies. Today,
open-face pizzas, stuffed calzones and
filled focaccias show the delicious evo-
lution of pizza from a bread to a meal.

Layered Pizza Pie

This delicious, easy-to-make pizza pie is a guaranteed winner! Choose either regular or hot Italian sausage, whichever suits your taste.

*2 cans (10 ounces each) refrigerated pizza
        dough*
$1/2$ pound bulk Italian sausage
1 medium onion, chopped (about $1/2$ cup)
1 clove garlic, finely chopped
1 can (8 ounces) pizza sauce (about 1 cup)
2 tablespoons sliced ripe olives
*$1^1/2$ cups shredded mozzarella cheese
        (6 ounces)*
*2 packages (10 ounces each) frozen
        chopped spinach, thawed and squeezed
        to drain*
1 teaspoon olive or vegetable oil
1 tablespoon grated Parmesan cheese

Heat oven to 400°. Lightly grease pie plate, $9 \times 1^1/4$ inches. Unroll 1 can of dough. Place dough in pie plate; press against bottom and side of pie plate to form crust.

Cook sausage, onion and garlic in 10-inch skillet over medium-high heat, stirring occasionally, until sausage is no longer pink; drain. Stir in pizza sauce and olives. Spoon sausage mixture onto dough in pie plate. Layer with $3/4$ cup of the mozzarella cheese, the spinach and remaining mozzarella cheese.

Unroll remaining can of dough. Press dough into 9-inch circle; place over filling. Pinch edges of dough together to seal; roll edge of dough up or flute to form rim. Cut several slits in dough. Brush with oil; sprinkle with Parmesan cheese. Bake 35 to 40 minutes or until deep golden brown. *6 servings.*

Nutrition Information Per Serving

1 serving		Percent of U.S. RDA	
Calories	455	Vitamin A	54%
Protein, g	24	Vitamin C	10%
Carbohydrate, g	49	Calcium	34%
Fat, g	20	Iron	26%
Cholesterol, mg	45		
Sodium, mg	1040		

Pizza Rustica

Rustic pizza pies, or focaccias, come from rural southern Italy. They are baked at a moderate heat to allow the ingredients inside to cook evenly, unlike pizza, which is cooked quickly at a high temperature.

Basic Pizza Dough for Two Crusts
   (page 32)
1 cup Simple Pizza Sauce (page 86) or
   purchased pizza sauce
¼ pound bulk Italian sausage, cooked and
   drained
1 cup shredded mozzarella cheese
   (4 ounces)
½ cup shredded provolone cheese
   (2 ounces)
½ cup sliced fresh mushrooms
½ cup finely chopped pepperoni or salami
   (about 3 ounces)
1 medium onion, thinly sliced
1 cup chopped fresh basil leaves
1 teaspoon olive or vegetable oil

Prepare Basic Pizza Dough and Simple Pizza Sauce.

Heat oven to 425°. Grease pie plate, 10×1½ inches. Divide dough in half. Press or roll one half into 13-inch circle on lightly floured surface; place in pie plate. Sprinkle sausage over dough in pie plate. Mix cheeses; sprinkle over sausage. Top with pizza sauce, mushrooms, pepperoni, onion and basil.

Press or roll remaining dough into 11-inch circle on lightly floured surface; place over filling. Pinch edges of dough together to seal; roll edge of dough up, forming a rim. Prick top of dough thoroughly with fork; brush with oil. Bake about 30 minutes or until golden brown. Serve hot or cold. *8 servings.*

Nutrition Information Per Serving

1 serving		Percent of U.S. RDA	
Calories	795	Vitamin A	22%
Protein, g	40	Vitamin C	30%
Carbohydrate, g	69	Calcium	40%
Fat, g	40	Iron	40%
Cholesterol, mg	140		
Sodium, mg	2010		

Pizza Rustica

Italian Cheeses and Herbs

Cheese

Italy produces a multitude of cheeses that vary according to region, climate and soil. Many small farms and individual families still produce some of the country's finest cheeses. Several cheeses, such as Parmesan, mozzarella, provolone and ricotta, have gained tremendous popularity in American cooking.

The most popular cheeses and their uses are listed below. Like wines, many cheeses carry names representing their region of origin or processing method.

Asiago: This sharp, dry cow's milk cheese originated in a plateau area near the city of Asiago. Asiago can be grated and sprinkled over pasta and vegetables.

Bel Paese: Literally translated, this means "nice country" and is a soft cow's milk cheese from Lombardy. Bel Paese is a great melting cheese and can be used in hot sandwiches and baked dishes. Italians serve this as a dessert cheese, often with fresh fruit.

Fontina: A semi-soft cow's milk cheese from the Piedmont region in northern Italy, Fontina has a delicate fruity flavor similar to the taste of Swiss, but Fontina has no holes. This cheese is ideal for melting and is used for fondues, stuffed pasta or meats and as a cheese for pizza. Appropriately named for its melting characteristics, Fontina means "little spring fountain."

Gorgonzola: This creamy, moist cheese similar to American blue cheese, but with a sharper flavor, originally came from the town of Gorgonzola, near Milan, in northern Italy. Its distinctive sharpness comes from the goat milk used in combination with cow's milk. This cheese can be crumbled on salads, added to creamy sauces for pasta or served for dessert with fresh pears.

Mascarpone: This very rich, soft cheese is smooth and mild and originated in northern Italy. Similar to cream cheese, it is ideal for sweet and savory spreads or for making cheese-based desserts. Mascarpone is the cheese used in the popular Italian dessert Tira Mi Su (see page 156).

Mozzarella: This is the most common Italian cheese that has been transplanted to America. Naples is the city of origin for this cow's milk cheese originally made with water buffalo milk. Most of the mozzarella available in the United States is the low-moisture, part-skim type sold in blocks or shredded with a characteristic chewy, stringy texture. Mozzarella is widely used as a pizza cheese, in sandwiches, pasta dishes and appetizers. Fresh mozzarella, a wonderful appetizer cheese, is white in color with a tender, smooth texture, and is becoming more widely available in delis and cheese shops.

Key to photograph on following page

Following pages: Herbs and Cheeses Frequently Used in Italian Cooking: (1) Romano (2) Italian Parsley (3) Parmesan (4) Ricotta (5) Mint (6) Basil (7) Watercress (8) Thyme (9) Rosemary (10) Provolone (11) Fontina (12) Asiago (13) Sage (14) Mozzarella (15) Gorgonzola (16) Swiss (17) Bel Paese (18) Oregano (19) Mascarpone (20) Marjoram

Parmesan: This hard cow's milk cheese is excellent for grating. Originally from the city of Parma, the finest and most authentic cheese has the "Parmigiano Reggiano" seal stamped on its hard rind and has a flaky, dry consistency when cut. Parmesan's most familiar form is the dry, grated variety sold in round, cardboard containers. It is also available pre-shredded and in wedges. Parmesan cheese and pasta are perfect partners, but Parmesan also is excellent in salads, as an appetizer with a glass of wine or flaked over cold cuts. Imported Parmesan has much more flavor and suitable texture than domestic varieties.

Provolone: This southern Italian cheese with a sharp flavor similar to, but stronger than, mozzarella takes many forms and sometimes has a stringlike texture. After it has aged, Provolone's flavor is more pungent and can be used for grating. Its rich, nutty taste and excellent melting quality make it an ideal partner with mozzarella when topping pizzas. Try smoked provolone paired with salami or ham in sandwiches.

Ricotta: This is a fresh and creamy soft cheese similar to cottage cheese, but with a sweeter flavor and no curds. Ricotta cheese retains its texture when heated, making it ideal for stuffing manicotti or as a layer in lasagna. Ricotta also is used in desserts such as Cannoli (see page 160) and cheesecake.

Romano: This dry, firm grating cheese made from sheep's milk is similar to Parmesan although saltier and more tangy. Romano is most often used just like Parmesan cheese or when a bolder flavor is desired.

Swiss: Why Swiss cheese in Italian cooking? The northern Alpine region of Italy borders Switzerland, connecting their cultures. Swiss is a hard cheese with a mild, nutty flavor recognized by its large holes or "eyes," which develop after the initial whey is removed and curds are heated and pressed. In Italy, it is favored for thick sauces and complements gnocchi dumplings especially well.

Herbs

Herbs and spices are the hallmarks of ethnic culinary identity, giving us a world of unique taste sensations and flavor combinations. Whether grown in pots on a sunny windowsill, in home gardens or purchased from a farmer's market or supermarket, fresh herbs enliven the food to which they're added. Fresh herbs are preferred, but when they just aren't available, you can substitute dried herbs. In most cases, 1 teaspoon of dried herbs can be used for 3 tablespoons of fresh.

Basil: Sweet, aromatic basil can be a flavor powerhouse. It is the preferred herb for tomato recipes and is a flavorful addition when tossed with fresh greens in a salad. In addition to being the classic herb in Pesto (see page 86), basil also finds its way into soups and appetizers.

Bay Leaves: Bay leaves are pungent and aromatic. Dried leaves are the most widely used form; however, Italians often use fresh bay leaves. Their assertive flavor goes well with grilled meats, soups and stews.

Chives: Delicate chive stems have a very mild onion flavor and bright green color. They are compatible with almost any food in which mild onion flavor is desired and are used extensively for garnishing.

Marjoram: Closely related to oregano, marjoram is moderately aromatic with a slightly bitter undertone. It can be added to most meat dishes, soups and vegetables or robust salad dressings.

Mint: Mint's distinctive sweet aroma, flavor and cool aftertaste make it suitable for soups, salads, fruit desserts and punches, as well as lamb and other meats.

Oregano: Oregano is strong and aromatic with a pleasantly bitter undertone. It combines perfectly with the sweetness of basil in sauces and soups or in meat and egg dishes.

Rosemary: Rosemary has a fresh, sweet flavor that can be very strong. It is excellent for poultry, lamb, seafood or in breads. Rosemary is the herb most often sprinkled and baked on focaccia bread.

Sage: Sage is aromatic and slightly bitter. Sage is well-suited for bread and meat stuffing, poultry, sausages and soups. A classic Italian sauce combines browned butter, fresh sage leaves and garlic and is tossed with angel-hair pasta or linguine.

Thyme: Thyme is aromatic and pungent; a little goes a long way. It is excellent with poultry, fish, seafood, bread and meat stuffing or with tomatoes.

Pesto-Salami Pizza

The contemporary combination of pesto and salami make this enticing pizza a spicy taste sensation.

Basic Pizza Dough for Two Crusts
   (page 32)
³/₄ cup Pesto (page 86) or purchased pesto
1 egg, beaten
1 cup shredded mozzarella cheese
   (4 ounces)
1 cup shredded provolone cheese
   (4 ounces)
1¹/₂ cups thinly sliced fresh mushrooms
   (about 4 ounces)
1 small onion, thinly sliced
¹/₄ pound thinly sliced salami

Prepare Basic Pizza Dough and Pesto.

Heat oven to 375°. Grease cookie sheet. Divide dough in half. Press one-half dough into 12-inch circle on cookie sheet with floured fingers; brush ¹/₂-inch edge of dough with egg. Spread Pesto on dough to within ¹/₂ inch of edge. Arrange cheeses, mushrooms, onion and salami on Pesto to within ¹/₂ inch of edge.

Press remaining dough into 12-inch circle on lightly floured surface; place over filling. Press edges of dough together with fingers or fork to seal; prick top of dough thoroughly with fork. Brush top with egg. Bake 20 to 30 minutes or until golden brown. *8 servings.*

Nutrition Information Per Serving

1 serving		Percent of U.S. RDA	
Calories	405	Vitamin A	10%
Protein, g	18	Vitamin C	10%
Carbohydrate, g	32	Calcium	26%
Fat, g	23	Iron	16%
Cholesterol, mg	60		
Sodium, mg	950		

Mediterranean Peppered Pizza

This boldly flavored pizza will delight vegetable pizza lovers and may even convert some die-hard meat fans!

*Basic Pizza Dough for Two Crusts
    (page 32)**
1 cup shredded mozzarella cheese
    (4 ounces)
1 jar (7 ounces) roasted red bell peppers,
    drained and diced (about ³/₄ cup)
1 jar (7 ounces) sun-dried tomatoes in oil,
    drained and chopped
2 roma tomatoes or 1 small tomato, sliced
1 small red onion, sliced
2 pepperoncini peppers, sliced
2 tablespoons sliced pimiento-stuffed
    olives
2 tablespoons sliced ripe olives
¹/₂ cup shredded mozzarella cheese
    (2 ounces)
1 tablespoon chopped fresh or 1 teaspoon
    dried basil leaves*

Prepare Basic Pizza Dough.

Heat oven to 425°. Grease cookie sheet or 12-inch pizza pan. Press dough into 12-inch circle on cookie sheet with floured fingers. Sprinkle with 1 cup of the cheese. Arrange all remaining ingredients, except ¹/₂ cup of the cheese and basil, over cheese. Sprinkle with remaining cheese and basil. Bake 15 to 20 minutes or until crust is golden brown. *8 servings.*

*Prepare Basic Pizza Dough as directed— except substitute 1 cup whole wheat flour for 1 cup of the all-purpose flour, if desired.

Nutrition Information Per Serving

1 serving		Percent of U.S. RDA	
Calories	200	Vitamin A	10%
Protein, g	9	Vitamin C	28%
Carbohydrate, g	34	Calcium	12%
Fat, g	5	Iron	12%
Cholesterol, mg	10		
Sodium, mg	430		

Fireworks Pizza

*1 purchased Italian bread shell
    (16 ounces) or baked 12-inch pizza
    crust
1 jar (12 ounces) pickled Giardiniera
    vegetable mix, well drained
1 tablespoon chopped drained
    pepperoncini peppers
1 cup crumbled feta cheese
2 teaspoons chopped fresh parsley or
    1 teaspoon dried parsley flakes*

Heat oven to 400°. Place bread shell on ungreased cookie sheet. Arrange vegetable mix and peppers evenly over bread shell. Sprinkle with cheese and parsley. Bake 10 to 12 minutes or until cheese is melted and bubbly. *8 servings.*

Nutrition Information Per Serving

1 serving		Percent of U.S. RDA	
Calories	300	Vitamin A	4%
Protein, g	8	Vitamin C	2%
Carbohydrate, g	45	Calcium	10%
Fat, g	11	Iron	14%
Cholesterol, mg	15		
Sodium, mg	840		

Calzone

A calzone is like a folded-over stuffed pizza; the circle of dough is folded in half over the filling and then sealed. During baking the filling plumps, stretching the dough somewhat until it resembles a "stuffed stocking," the literal translation of calzone.

Basic Pizza Dough for One Crust
  (page 32)
¹/₃ cup Simple Pizza Sauce (page 86) or
  purchased pizza sauce
¹/₄ cup shredded mozzarella cheese
  (1 ounce)
¹/₄ cup shredded provolone cheese
  (1 ounce)
¹/₄ cup chopped fully cooked smoked ham
  or prosciutto (about 1¹/₂ ounces)
¹/₄ cup chopped pepperoni or salami
  (about 1¹/₂ ounces)
2 tablespoons chopped fresh basil leaves

Prepare Basic Pizza Dough and Simple Pizza Sauce.

Heat oven to 375°. Grease cookie sheet. Press dough into 12-inch circle on cookie sheet with floured fingers. Mix cheeses; place *on half of* circle to within 1 inch of edge. Mix ham and salami; sprinkle over cheeses. Pour pizza sauce over ham and salami. Sprinkle with basil.

Lift and gently stretch dough over filling; press edges of dough together with fingers or fork to seal. Cut slit in top. Bake 20 to 25 minutes or until golden brown. *2 servings.*

Nutrition Information Per Serving

1 serving		Percent of U.S. RDA	
Calories	630	Vitamin A	12%
Protein, g	33	Vitamin C	20%
Carbohydrate, g	66	Calcium	34%
Fat, g	26	Iron	32%
Cholesterol, mg	70		
Sodium, mg	1720		

Savory Chicken Wedges

This bistro-style sandwich is perfect for casual entertaining.

2 tablespoons olive or vegetable oil
2 cloves garlic, finely chopped
2 green onions, chopped
1 pound boneless, skinless chicken breasts, cut into 1-inch pieces
1 tablespoon chopped fresh or 1 teaspoon dried basil leaves
1 tablespoon chopped fresh parsley or 1 teaspoon dried parsley flakes
¼ teaspoon salt
¼ teaspoon pepper
1 purchased Italian bread shell (16 ounces) or baked 12-inch pizza crust
2 tablespoons sliced pimiento-stuffed olives
2 tablespoons sliced ripe olives
¾ cup shredded mozzarella cheese (3 ounces)
¼ cup freshly shredded Parmesan cheese

Heat oven to 400°. Heat oil in 10-inch skillet over medium heat. Cook garlic, onions and chicken in oil 6 to 8 minutes, stirring frequently, until chicken is no longer pink in center. Stir in basil, parsley, salt and pepper.

Place bread shell on ungreased cookie sheet. Spoon chicken mixture onto bread shell. Top with olives. Sprinkle with cheeses. Bake 10 to 12 minutes or until cheese is melted and bubbly. Cut into wedges. *8 servings.*

Nutrition Information Per Serving

1 serving		Percent of U.S. RDA	
Calories	345	Vitamin A	2%
Protein, g	21	Vitamin C	*
Carbohydrate, g	34	Calcium	14%
Fat, g	15	Iron	16%
Cholesterol, mg	40		
Sodium, mg	820		

Pesto-Chicken Sandwich

1 tablespoon olive or vegetable oil
1 medium stalk celery, chopped (about ¹/₂ cup)
1 cup cut-up cooked chicken
¹/₃ cup Pesto (page 86) or purchased pesto
2 purchased Italian bread shells, 6 to 8 inches in diameter (8 ounces)
2 tablespoons freshly shredded Parmesan cheese
¹/₂ cup shredded lettuce

Heat oil in 10-inch skillet over medium-high heat. Cook celery in oil 4 to 5 minutes, stirring occasionally, until crisp-tender; reduce heat. Stir in chicken and pesto. Cook, stirring occasionally, until hot.

Spoon chicken mixture onto bread shells. Mix cheese and lettuce; sprinkle over chicken mixture. Cut each bread shell in half. *4 servings.*

Nutrition Information Per Serving

1 serving		Percent of U.S. RDA	
Calories	295	Vitamin A	2%
Protein, g	15	Vitamin C	*
Carbohydrate, g	16	Calcium	12%
Fat, g	19	Iron	12%
Cholesterol, mg	35		
Sodium, mg	250		

Italian Bread Well

This fun sandwich uses Italian bread to make a "well" that is then stuffed with a zesty tuna salad. Save the bread you hollow out to make croutons for your next salad.

2 cans (6 ¹/₈ ounces each) tuna in water, drained
1 large tomato, seeded and chopped (about 1 cup)
2 green onions, chopped
¹/₂ cup creamy Italian dressing
1 tablespoon chopped fresh or 1 teaspoon dried basil leaves
1 tablespoon chopped fresh parsley or 1 teaspoon dried parsley flakes
¹/₄ teaspoon salt
¹/₈ teaspoon pepper
1 unsliced round loaf Italian or Vienna bread (8 to 10 inches in diameter)

Mix all ingredients except bread until well blended. Cut 1-inch slice from top of bread loaf; set aside. Remove bread from center of loaf, leaving 1-inch shell on side and bottom. Spoon tuna mixture into bread shell. Replace top slice of bread. Cut into wedges. *4 servings.*

Nutrition Information Per Serving

1 serving		Percent of U.S. RDA	
Calories	400	Vitamin A	6%
Protein, g	30	Vitamin C	8%
Carbohydrate, g	38	Calcium	6%
Fat, g	15	Iron	26%
Cholesterol, mg	15		
Sodium, mg	1000		

Pesto-Chicken Sandwich

3

Pasta and Sauces

Manicotti (page 72); Garlic and Romaine Salad (page 147)

51

Egg Noodles

3 cups all-purpose flour or semolina
4 jumbo eggs
1/4 teaspoon salt
1 teaspoon olive or vegetable oil

Place flour in a mound on surface or in large bowl. Make a well in center of flour; add remaining ingredients. Mix thoroughly with fork, gradually bringing flour to center, until dough forms. (If dough is too sticky, gradually add flour when kneading. If dough is too dry, mix in enough water to make dough easy to handle.) Knead on lightly floured surface about 15 minutes or until smooth and elastic. Cover with plastic wrap or aluminum foil. Let stand 15 minutes.

Divide dough into 4 equal parts. (If desired, wrap unrolled dough securely and refrigerate up to 2 days. Let stand uncovered at room temperature 30 minutes before rolling and cutting.) Roll and cut as directed (right) for Hand Rolling or Manual Pasta Machine.

Arrange noodles in single layer on lightly floured towels; sprinkle lightly with all-purpose flour. (Or hang noodles on rack.) Let stand uncovered at room temperature 30 minutes.* Cook immediately as directed below, or cover fresh noodles and refrigerate up to 2 days, arranged in single layer on lightly floured towels.

Heat 4 quarts water to boiling in 6- to 8-quart saucepan; add noodles. Boil uncovered 2 to 4 minutes, stirring occasionally, until *al dente* (tender but firm). Begin testing for doneness when noodles rise to surface of water. Drain noodles. Do not rinse. *24 ounces uncooked noodles.*

*If not using pasta immediately, toss fresh pasta lightly with flour. Allow to stand until

partially dry but still pliable; loosely coil pasta into rounds for easier storage. Store in sealed plastic container or plastic bags for up to 3 days or freeze up to 1 month.

HAND ROLLING: Roll 1 part dough with rolling pin into rectangle 1/8 to 1/16 inch thick on lightly floured surface (keep remaining dough covered). Sprinkle dough lightly with all-purpose flour. Loosely fold rectangle lengthwise into thirds; cut crosswise into 1 1/2- to 2-inch strips for wide noodles, 1/4-inch strips for fettuccine or 1/8-inch strips for linguine. Shake out strips. Repeat with remaining dough.

MANUAL PASTA MACHINE: Flatten 1 part dough with hands to 1/2-inch thickness on lightly floured surface (keep remaining dough covered). Feed 1 part dough through smooth rollers set at widest setting. Sprinkle with all-purpose flour if dough becomes sticky. Fold lengthwise into thirds. Repeat feeding dough through rollers and folding into thirds 8 to 10 times or until firm and smooth. Feed dough through progressively narrower settings until dough is 1/8 to 1/16 inch thick. (Dough will lengthen as it becomes thinner; it can be cut crosswise at any time for easier handling.) Feed dough through cutting rollers of desired shape. To cut by hand, sprinkle dough lightly with all-purpose flour; cut into 1/4-inch strips for fettuccine or 1/8-inch strips for linguine. Repeat with remaining dough.

HALF-RECIPE EGG NOODLES: Cut all ingredients in half. Continue as directed.

Nutrition Information Per Serving

1 serving		Percent of U.S. RDA	
Calories	145	Vitamin A	2%
Protein, g	6	Vitamin C	*
Carbohydrate, g	24	Calcium	2%
Fat, g	3	Iron	10%
Cholesterol, mg	90		
Sodium, mg	70		

Spinach Noodles

*1 package (10 ounces) frozen chopped
    spinach
3 cups all-purpose flour or semolina
3 large eggs
$1/4$ teaspoon salt*

Cook spinach as directed on package; squeeze or press out liquid. Finely chop spinach, or place in food processor or blender, cover and process until smooth.

Place flour in a mound on surface or in large bowl. Make a well in center of flour; add spinach, eggs and salt. Mix thoroughly with fork, gradually bringing flour to center, until dough forms. (If dough is too sticky, gradually add flour when kneading. If dough is too dry, mix in enough water to make dough easy to handle.) Knead on lightly floured surface about 15 minutes or until smooth and elastic. Cover with plastic wrap or aluminum foil. Let stand 15 minutes.

Divide dough into 4 equal parts. (If desired, wrap unrolled dough securely and refrigerate up to 2 days. Let stand at room temperature 30 minutes before rolling and cutting.) Roll and cut as directed (right) for Hand Rolling or Manual Pasta Machine.

Arrange noodles in single layer on lightly floured towels; sprinkle lightly with all-purpose flour. (Or hang noodles on rack.) Let stand uncovered at room temperature 30 minutes.* Cook immediately as directed (right), or cover fresh noodles and refrigerate up to 2 days, arranged in single layer on lightly floured towels.

Heat 4 quarts water to boiling in 6- to 8-quart saucepan; add noodles. Boil uncovered 2 to 4 minutes, stirring occasionally, until *al dente* (tender but firm). Begin testing for doneness when noodles rise to surface of water. Drain noodles. Do not rinse. *24 ounces uncooked noodles.*

*If not using pasta immediately, toss fresh pasta lightly with flour. Allow to stand until partially dry but still pliable; loosely coil pasta into rounds for easier storage. Store in sealed plastic container or plastic bags for up to 3 days or freeze up to 1 month.

HAND ROLLING: Roll 1 part dough with rolling pin into rectangle $1/8$ to $1/16$ inch thick on lightly floured surface (keep remaining dough covered). Sprinkle dough lightly with all-purpose flour. Loosely fold rectangle lengthwise into thirds; cut crosswise into $1/4$-inch strips for fettuccine, $1/8$-inch strips for linguine. Shake out strips. Repeat with remaining dough.

MANUAL PASTA MACHINE: Flatten 1 part dough with hands to $1/2$-inch thickness on lightly floured surface (keep remaining dough covered). Feed 1 part dough through smooth rollers set at widest setting. Sprinkle with all-purpose flour if dough becomes sticky. Fold lengthwise into thirds. Repeat feeding dough through rollers and folding into thirds 8 to 10 times or until firm and smooth. Feed dough through progressively narrower settings until dough is $1/8$ to $1/16$ inch thick. (Dough will lengthen as it becomes thinner; it can be cut crosswise at any time for easier handling.) Feed dough through cutting rollers of desired shape. To cut by hand, sprinkle dough lightly with all-purpose flour; cut into $1/4$-inch strips for fettuccine, $1/8$-inch strips for linguine. Repeat with remaining dough.

Nutrition Information Per Serving

1 serving		Percent of U.S. RDA	
Calories	140	Vitamin A	14%
Protein, g	5	Vitamin C	*
Carbohydrate, g	25	Calcium	2%
Fat, g	2	Iron	10%
Cholesterol, mg	60		
Sodium, mg	75		

Spaghetti and Meatballs

To make short work of forming meatballs, use a spring-loaded cookie scoop instead of shaping each one by hand.

1 can (16 ounces) whole tomatoes,
*   undrained*
1 can (8 ounces) tomato sauce
1 large onion, chopped (about 1 cup)
1 clove garlic, crushed
1 teaspoon sugar
1 teaspoon dried oregano leaves
³/₄ teaspoon salt
³/₄ teaspoon dried basil leaves
¹/₂ teaspoon dried marjoram leaves
Meatballs (right)
6 cups hot cooked spaghetti

Mix all ingredients except Meatballs and spaghetti in 3-quart saucepan; break up tomatoes. Heat to boiling; reduce heat. Cover and simmer 30 minutes, stirring occasionally.

Prepare Meatballs. Stir meatballs into tomato mixture. Cover and simmer 30 minutes, stirring occasionally. Serve over spaghetti and, if desired, with grated Parmesan cheese. *6 servings.*

MEATBALLS

1 pound ground beef
¹/₂ cup dry bread crumbs
¹/₄ cup milk
¹/₂ teaspoon salt
¹/₂ teaspoon Worcestershire sauce
¹/₄ teaspoon pepper
1 small onion, chopped (about ¹/₄ cup)
1 egg

Heat oven to 400°. Mix all ingredients. Shape into twenty 1¹/₂-inch meatballs. Place in ungreased rectangular pan, 13 × 9 × 2 inches. Bake uncovered 20 to 25 minutes or until no longer pink in center; drain.

TO PANFRY: Cook meatballs in 10-inch skillet over medium heat about 20 minutes, turning occasionally, until no longer pink in center; drain.

Nutrition Information Per Serving

1 serving		Percent of U.S. RDA	
Calories	365	Vitamin A	10%
Protein, g	22	Vitamin C	16%
Carbohydrate, g	44	Calcium	8%
Fat, g	13	Iron	22%
Cholesterol, mg	80		
Sodium, mg	1050		

Spaghetti Puttanesca

The ladies of the night in Naples are credited with inventing this dish. They liked it because it's fast, easy to cook, and uses a few inexpensive ingredients. We think you'll like it too!

$1/3$ cup olive or vegetable oil
2 cloves garlic, cut in half
1 tablespoon capers
4 flat fillets of anchovy in oil, drained
2 cans (28 ounces each) whole Italian-style tomatoes, drained and chopped
1 small red jalapeño chili, seeded and finely chopped
$1/2$ cup sliced imported Kalamata or ripe olives
1 package (16 ounces) spaghetti

Heat oil in Dutch oven or large saucepan over medium-high heat. Cook garlic in oil, stirring frequently until golden. Remove garlic and discard. Stir capers, anchovy fillets, tomatoes and chili into oil in Dutch oven. Heat to boiling; reduce heat. Simmer uncovered 20 minutes. Stir in olives; keep warm.

Cook spaghetti as directed on package; drain. Stir spaghetti into tomato mixture. Cook over high heat 3 minutes, stirring occasionally. *4 servings.*

Nutrition Information Per Serving

1 serving		Percent of U.S. RDA	
Calories	695	Vitamin A	36%
Protein, g	20	Vitamin C	68%
Carbohydrate, g	110	Calcium	14%
Fat, g	23	Iron	44%
Cholesterol, mg	5		
Sodium, mg	1400		

Chicken Tetrazzini

7 ounces uncooked spaghetti, broken in half
$1/4$ cup ($1/2$ stick) margarine or butter
$1/4$ cup all-purpose flour
$1/2$ teaspoon salt
$1/4$ teaspoon pepper
1 cup chicken broth
1 cup whipping (heavy) cream
2 tablespoons dry sherry or chicken broth
2 cups cubed cooked chicken
1 can (4 ounces) sliced mushrooms, drained
$1/2$ cup grated Parmesan cheese

Heat oven to 350°. Cook spaghetti as directed on package; drain. Melt margarine in 3-quart saucepan over low heat. Stir in flour, salt and pepper. Cook, stirring constantly, until smooth and bubbly; remove from heat. Stir in broth and whipping cream. Heat to boiling, stirring constantly. Boil and stir 1 minute. Stir in sherry, spaghetti, chicken and mushrooms.

Spoon into greased 2-quart casserole. Sprinkle with cheese. Bake uncovered about 30 minutes or until bubbly in center. *6 servings.*

Nutrition Information Per Serving

1 serving		Percent of U.S. RDA	
Calories	480	Vitamin A	24%
Protein, g	23	Vitamin C	*
Carbohydrate, g	34	Calcium	14%
Fat, g	28	Iron	14%
Cholesterol, mg	100		
Sodium, mg	780		

Spaghetti Carbonara

Coal miners are said to have invented this hearty and quick pasta dish—"carbonara" means coal miner in Italian.

1 package (16 ounces) spaghetti
1 clove garlic, finely chopped
6 slices bacon, cut into 1-inch pieces
³/₄ cup cholesterol-free egg product
1 tablespoon olive or vegetable oil
¹/₄ cup freshly grated Parmesan cheese
¹/₄ cup freshly grated Romano cheese
2 tablespoons chopped fresh parsley
¹/₄ teaspoon pepper
Freshly grated Parmesan cheese, if
*   desired*
Freshly ground pepper, if desired

Cook spaghetti as directed on package. Meanwhile, cook garlic and bacon, stirring occasionally, until bacon is crisp; drain. Mix egg product, olive oil, ¹/₄ cup Parmesan cheese, the Romano cheese, parsley and ¹/₄ teaspoon pepper; reserve.

Drain spaghetti and immediately return to saucepan over very low heat. Toss spaghetti quickly with egg product mixture. Toss in bacon-garlic mixture. Serve with pepper. *6 servings.*

Nutrition Information Per Serving

1 serving		Percent of U.S. RDA	
Calories	390	Vitamin A	4%
Protein, g	19	Vitamin C	2%
Carbohydrate, g	62	Calcium	18%
Fat, g	8	Iron	20%
Cholesterol, mg	15		
Sodium, mg	650		

Flour

Semolina flour is made from durum wheat, a hard wheat high in protein. When ground, it is yellow and has a coarse consistency similar to granulated sugar. Semolina is an excellent choice when making pasta because it gives structure and elasticity to the pasta dough, allows the dough to dry faster and is more tender and less gummy when cooked. Pasta dough made with semolina is slightly drier and stiffer than dough made with other flours because it absorbs liquid more easily— if the dough becomes too dry, add water a small bit at a time, until it holds together and is easy to handle. The dough should be allowed to rest after kneading so that it is easier to roll out. The resting period is an absolute necessity when using a rolling pin, but also is helpful if using a pasta machine.

If semolina flour is not available, or if you are making pasta dough for the first time, all-purpose flour also produces excellent pasta. The dough is less stiff and easier to handle. The amount of liquid you need varies slightly, depending on the dryness of the flour as well as the temperature and humidity of your kitchen. If the dough is dry and crumbly, add water a small amount at a time until the dough is easy to handle, but not too sticky.

Spaghetti Carbonara

Vermicelli with Fresh Herbs

1 package (16 ounces) vermicelli
¹/₄ cup olive or vegetable oil
2 tablespoons chopped pine nuts
1 tablespoon chopped fresh parsley
1 tablespoon capers, chopped
*2 teaspoons chopped fresh rosemary
    leaves*
2 teaspoons chopped fresh sage leaves
1 teaspoon chopped fresh basil leaves
1 pint cherry tomatoes, cut into fourths
Freshly ground pepper

Cook vermicelli as directed on package; drain. Meanwhile, mix oil, pine nuts, parsley, capers, rosemary, sage and basil in medium bowl. Stir in tomatoes. Mix vermicelli and herb mixture. Serve with pepper. *6 servings.*

Nutrition Information Per Serving

1 serving		Percent of U.S. RDA	
Calories	395	Vitamin A	4%
Protein, g	11	Vitamin C	10%
Carbohydrate, g	64	Calcium	2%
Fat, g	12	Iron	20%
Cholesterol, mg	0		
Sodium, mg	310		

Angel-hair Pasta in Garlic Sauce

Want a more subtle garlic flavor? Try mild-flavored elephant garlic in this sauce.

*1 package (16 ounces) capellini
    (angel-hair) pasta*
¹/₄ cup olive or vegetable oil
¹/₄ cup chopped fresh parsley
4 cloves garlic, finely chopped
¹/₂ cup freshly grated Parmesan cheese
Freshly ground pepper

Cook pasta as directed on package. Meanwhile, heat oil in 10-inch skillet over medium-high heat. Cook parsley and garlic in oil, stirring frequently, until garlic is soft. Drain pasta; mix with garlic mixture. Sprinkle with cheese. Serve with pepper. *6 servings.*

Nutrition Information Per Serving

1 serving		Percent of U.S. RDA	
Calories	400	Vitamin A	2%
Protein, g	13	Vitamin C	2%
Carbohydrate, g	62	Calcium	10%
Fat, g	12	Iron	18%
Cholesterol, mg	5		
Sodium, mg	430		

Vermicelli with Fresh Herbs

Angel-hair Pasta with Shrimp

1 package (16 ounces) capellini
  (angel-hair) pasta
¹/₄ cup olive or vegetable oil
2 tablespoons chopped fresh parsley
2 cloves garlic, finely chopped
1 small red jalapeño chili, seeded and
  finely chopped
¹/₃ cup dry white wine or chicken broth
¹/₂ teaspoon freshly grated nutmeg
12 ounces frozen peeled raw small shrimp,
  thawed

Cook pasta as directed on package. Meanwhile, heat oil in Dutch oven or 12-inch skillet over medium-high heat. Cook parsley, garlic and chili in oil, stirring frequently, until garlic is soft. Stir in wine, nutmeg and shrimp; reduce heat. Cover and simmer about 5 minutes or until shrimp are pink.

Drain pasta; toss with shrimp mixture in 3-quart saucepan. Cook over medium heat 2 minutes, stirring occasionally. *4 servings.*

Nutrition Information Per Serving

1 serving		Percent of U.S. RDA	
Calories	615	Vitamin A	16%
Protein, g	28	Vitamin C	22%
Carbohydrate, g	93	Calcium	6%
Fat, g	16	Iron	38%
Cholesterol, mg	120		
Sodium, mg	600		

Linguine with Clam Sauce

Egg Noodles (page 52)*
Clam Sauce (page 88)
4 quarts water
Chopped fresh parsley

Prepare dough for Egg Noodles; cut into linguine as directed. Remove one-third of the linguine and store for another use. Prepare Clam Sauce; keep warm.

Heat water to boiling in 6- to 8-quart saucepan; add linguine. Boil uncovered 2 to 4 minutes, stirring occasionally, until *al dente* (tender but firm). Begin testing for doneness when linguine rises to surface of water. Drain linguine. Do not rinse. Mix linguine and sauce. Sprinkle with parsley. *4 servings.*

* 1 package (16 ounces) fresh or dried linguine can be substituted for the Egg Noodles. Cook as directed on package.

Nutrition Information Per Serving

1 serving		Percent of U.S. RDA	
Calories	530	Vitamin A	40%
Protein, g	28	Vitamin C	58%
Carbohydrate, g	62	Calcium	14%
Fat, g	21	Iron	100%

Linguine with Clam Sauce

Linguine with Sugo Sauce

Egg Noodles (page 52)*
Sugo Sauce (page 82) or 4¹/₂ cups
purchased spaghetti sauce
4 quarts water
2 tablespoons freshly grated Parmesan
cheese

Prepare dough for Egg Noodles; cut into linguine as directed. Remove one-third of the linguine and store for another use. Prepare Sugo Sauce; keep warm.

Heat water to boiling in 6- to 8-quart saucepan; add linguine. Boil uncovered 2 to 4 minutes, stirring occasionally, until *al dente* (tender but firm). Begin testing for doneness when linguine rises to surface of water. Drain linguine. Do not rinse. Mix linguine and sauce. Sprinkle with cheese. *4 servings.*

*1 package (16 ounces) fresh or dried linguine can be substituted for the Egg Noodles. Cook as directed on package.

Nutrition Information Per Serving

1 serving		Percent of U.S. RDA	
Calories	415	Vitamin A	32%
Protein, g	17	Vitamin C	52%
Carbohydrate, g	70	Calcium	22%
Fat, g	11	Iron	40%
Cholesterol, mg	185		
Sodium, mg	1120		

Fettuccine Alfredo

Alfredo's was a popular restaurant in Rome, where the chef's fresh pasta was served at the table and topped with sauces prepared before the diner's eyes. Cream and Parmesan form one of the most versatile sauces for pasta, and this sauce from Alfredo's, served over fettuccine, has become known as Fettuccine Alfredo.

Egg Noodles (page 52)*
2 tablespoons margarine or butter
1¹/₂ cups whipping (heavy) cream or half-and-half
1 tablespoon all-purpose flour
¹/₄ teaspoon salt
¹/₈ teaspoon pepper
2 tablespoons freshly grated Parmesan
cheese
¹/₂ teaspoon freshly grated nutmeg
4 quarts water
2 tablespoons freshly grated Parmesan
cheese
Freshly grated nutmeg, if desired
Freshly ground pepper

Prepare dough for Egg Noodles; cut into fettuccine as directed. Remove one-third of the fettuccine and store for another use.

Melt margarine in 3-quart saucepan over medium-high heat. Mix whipping cream, flour, salt and pepper until smooth; pour into saucepan. Heat to boiling. Boil 1 minute, stirring frequently with wire whisk; remove from heat. Stir in 2 tablespoons cheese and ¹/₂ teaspoon nutmeg.

Heat water to boiling in 6- to 8-quart saucepan; add fettuccine. Boil uncovered 2 to 4 minutes, stirring occasionally, until *al dente* (tender but firm). Begin testing for doneness when fettuccine rise to surface of water. Drain fettuccine. Do not rinse. Mix fettuccine and sauce. Sprinkle with 2 tablespoons cheese and nutmeg. Serve with pepper. *4 servings.*

*1 package (16 ounces) fresh or dried fettuccine can be substituted for the Egg Noodles. Cook as directed on package

Nutrition Information Per Serving

1 serving		Percent of U.S. RDA	
Calories	795	Vitamin A	38%
Protein, g	19	Vitamin C	*
Carbohydrate, g	78	Calcium	18%
Fat, g	45	Iron	28%
Cholesterol, mg	230		
Sodium, mg	370		

Fettuccine alla "Bravo!"

A beautifully seasoned tomato sauce mixes with whipping cream for a unique and satisfying twist on Fettuccine Alfredo.

4 cups Sugo Sauce (page 82) or purchased spaghetti sauce
Egg Noodles (page 52)*
1 tablespoon margarine or butter
1 cup sliced fresh mushrooms
¹/₂ cup chopped fully cooked smoked ham or prosciutto (about 3 ounces)
2 green onions, thinly sliced
1 cup whipping (heavy) cream
¹/₂ teaspoon freshly grated nutmeg
¹/₂ teaspoon pepper
4 quarts water
¹/₂ cup freshly grated Parmesan cheese

Prepare Sugo Sauce. Prepare dough for Egg Noodles; cut into fettuccine as directed. Remove one-third of the fettuccine and store for another use.

Melt margarine in 3-quart saucepan over medium-high heat. Cook mushrooms, ham and onions in margarine, stirring frequently, until mushrooms are soft. Stir in whipping cream, nutmeg and pepper. Heat to boiling; reduce heat. Simmer uncovered about 20 minutes, stirring frequently, until thickened. Stir in Sugo Sauce. Heat to boiling; reduce heat. Simmer uncovered 10 minutes, stirring occasionally.

Heat water to boiling in 6- to 8-quart saucepan; add fettuccine. Boil uncovered 2 to 4 minutes, stirring occasionally, until *al dente* (tender but firm). Begin testing for doneness when fettuccine rises to surface of water. Drain fettuccine. Do not rinse. Mix fettuccine and sauce. Sprinkle with cheese. *6 servings.*

* 1 package (16 ounces) fresh or dried fettuccine can be substituted for the Egg Noodles. Cook as directed on package.

Nutrition Information Per Serving

1 serving		Percent of U.S. RDA	
Calories	460	Vitamin A	32%
Protein, g	17	Vitamin C	32%
Carbohydrate, g	47	Calcium	26%
Fat, g	25	Iron	28%
Cholesterol, mg	185		
Sodium, mg	920		

All About Pasta

Pasta used to mean just spaghetti, lasagne or noodles, but now it is so much more! From dried to fresh, short to long, curly to ridged and flat to tubular, the tremendous variety available is certainly worth exploring.

To guide you through the plethora of enticing "pastabilities," we've identified the historical origins and names given to particular varieties. Like most Italian foods, pasta names have specific meanings representative of the shape or the intended use for preferred dishes. Despite similarity in shape, some varieties were originally referred to by different names depending on regional traditions.

Until the nineteenth century, Italian noodles were always manufactured during the summer and dried in the sun. When natural gas became available, hundreds of pasta factories throughout Italy began using gas-fired machines to dry dough, and pasta became available all year round. With the increased production, pasta was inexpensively exported to other countries.

- Most dried pasta doubles in size when cooked. Egg noodles are the exception and remain the same.
- When preparing pasta, allow $^{1}/_{2}$ to $^{3}/_{4}$ cup cooked pasta per side or appetizer serving. If you plan to make pasta your main entrée, allow $1^{1}/_{4}$ to $1^{1}/_{2}$ cups per serving.

- 1 ounce of dried pasta yields approximately $^{1}/_{2}$ cup of cooked pasta. This yield varies slightly depending on the shape, type and size of pasta.
- To easily measure 4 ounces of spaghetti, make a circle with your thumb and index finger, about the size of a quarter, and fill it with pasta.

The Different Types of Pasta

Bucatini: This is a long, hollow noodle, thicker than spaghetti, that originated in Naples. "Bucato" literally means "with a hole." When broken into thirds and served with a sauce, this noodle absorbs the flavor inwardly, adding more flavor to each bite.

Cannelloni (Manicotti): This large, 4-inch tubular noodle is usually stuffed and baked. Derived from the word "canna," cannelloni means "hollow cane."

Capellini (Angel-hair): Capellini means "thin hair," and is one of the thinnest cut spaghetti noodles. Legend has it that Parmesan cheese clings to this pasta like gold clings to angels' hair. It is a very quick pasta to prepare because it needs to boil only a few minutes and is best served with light sauces and in soups.

Ditalini: This pasta is cut into short segments resembling thimbles. Two types are available: lisci or smooth, appropriate for soups and salads; or regati, meaning grooved, which is suitable for chunky sauces. Typically, it is cooked in soups or served with a vegetable sauce.

Farfalle (Bow-ties): Traditionally, this bow-tie shaped pasta is accompanied by colorful sauces, reminiscent of blooming gardens, with fresh herbs or ripe vegetables such as sweet bell peppers or zucchini. Miniature bow-ties are known as Tripolini and are appropriate for soups or salads.

Fettuccine: Literally meaning "little strands," fettuccine is a long, flat noodle, usually ¼ inch wide. Thick, smooth white sauces, such as Alfredo, cling beautifully to this pasta. Fettuccine is available in many flavors including plain and spinach.

Fusilli: This long or short curled pasta from southern Italy usually is served with spicy tomato sauces. Hailing originally from Naples, it also is known as "Eliche" or "propellers," for its quality of trapping particles of the sauce and "propelling" them to the tongue.

(continued on page 68)

Following pages: Types of Pasta: (1) Vermicelli (2) Capellini (Angel-hair) (3) Rotini (4) Fusilli (5) Bucatini (6) Mafalde (7) Rigatoni (8) Lasagne (9) Orecchiette (10) Rosamarina (Orzo) (11) Farfalle (Bow-ties) (12) Gnocchi (13) Ziti (14) Baby Bow-ties (15) Penne (16) Ditalini (17) Medium Shells (18) Tortellini (19) Small Shells (20) Ravioli (21) Fettucine

Gnocchi: Gnocchi refers to any of several soft dumplings made from boiled potatoes, eggs and flour. Gnocchi means "lumps," because of the irregular, somewhat craggy shapes these dumplings have when cooked in soups. They range from marble to golf ball size, and are boiled and served with bitter or cream-based sauces.

Linguine: This is a flat, thin noodle served with light sauces such as clam or pesto. The name means "little tongues" because its original shape resembled the thickness of a songbird's tongue.

Mafalde (mini-lasagne noodles): This is a long, flat, narrow noodle with curled edges, popular for sauces with seafood. Mafalde also is available in a short length and often is referred to as mini-lasagne noodles.

Penne: Penne is a short cut pasta about $1\frac{1}{4}$ inches long. Tubular in shape with slanted cuts at both ends, penne can have a smooth or grooved finish. The word "penne" means "feather," indicating either the lightness of the noodle, or the transversely cut shape, which resembles a wing of a bird. It is excellent with tomato and vegetable sauces.

Ravioli: This pillow-shaped pasta popular in several Italian regions is usually made with a stuffing of spinach and cheese. Ravioli also are filled with ingredients such as crabmeat or pumpkin. Traditionally served with butter or Parmesan, this pasta also is delicious with tomato and meat sauces. Due to its richness, ravioli usually is served as a main course or on special occasions.

Rigatoni: This is a short cut, wide tubular pasta with lengthwise grooves, about 1 inch long. It suits most chunky sauces and meat sauces.

Rosamarina (Orzo): So named for its resemblance to rice, this pasta is ideal in soups, salads and side dishes.

Rotini: This short cut pasta with a corkscrew shape is sold plain or tricolored. A wider version of this shape is called rotelle. Rotini is a favorite for salads.

Shells: Shells are available in jumbo, medium and small sizes. Jumbo shells are great stuffed, whereas medium and small shells are more suited for thick sauces, soups and salads.

Tortelli: Tortelli is a round form of ravioli, which literally translated means "little torte." Usually cut into a shape resembling a shiny sun, tortelli also can have a half-moon shape. This pasta usually is served with light sauces so that the flavor of the filling can come through.

Tortellini: These little rings of pasta filled with cheese originated in the city of Bologna. Both plain and spinach-flavored tortellini are available, and fresh, refrigerated tortellini is offered with a variety of fillings such as Italian sausage or chicken. It is usually served with a tomato or cream sauce. Tortellini is also well-suited to soups and salads. To prevent tortellini from losing its shape and filling, do not overcook it.

Vermicelli: This is a long, very thin pasta. "Little worms" is the original meaning of this word, which describes the squirming motion the noodles undergo when surrounded by sauce and twirled around a fork. Vermicelli was the original pasta for spaghetti and meatballs, and it is well-suited for use with lighter sauces and in soups.

Ziti: This short cut, 2-inch tubular noodle with a smooth surface goes well with chunky sauces and meat sauces.

Pasta Pointers

Cooking Pasta: Follow these tips for perfect *al dente* pasta.

1. Use 1 gallon (4 quarts) of water for each pound of pasta so that pasta cooks uniformly.
2. Adding oil isn't necessary to cook pasta properly. Sauces cling much better to noodles boiled in water with no oil.
3. Water should always be at a full boil when pasta is added and should remain at boiling during the entire cooking time.
4. Avoid over-cooking pasta. Over-cooked pasta is mushy and pasty. Follow recipe directions carefully. Pasta should be cooked *al dente*, or firm to the bite.
5. Never rinse pasta after draining, unless making a cold pasta dish. After draining, immediately mix warm pasta with sauce and serve immediately.

Draining Noodles: Draining noodles is an important step in preparing pasta dishes because it instantly stops the cooking. Draining should be done quickly, to prevent noodles from sticking together or cooling down. If the recipe calls for it, you can add some Parmesan cheese while mixing the noodles and sauce, to help sauce cling to the noodles. Don't add oil or rinse noodles in cold water (unless you are making a pasta salad) because this cools the noodles and makes them too slippery for a sauce to cling to.

Reheating Cooked Pasta: Leftover pasta can be tossed with a small amount of oil and refrigerated in a resealable plastic bag or covered container for up to 3 days. To reheat, place the pasta in boiling water for several minutes, or place in colander and pour boiling water over it until hot. Drain and use immediately.

Pasta Storage: Dried pasta can be stored indefinitely in your pantry. Purchased fresh pasta should be used before the expiration date printed on the package. To store homemade pasta, see page 52.

Straw and Hay Pasta

The "straw" in this delightful dish is the egg noodles; the "hay" is the green spinach noodles. To make this dish super simple, make it with store-bought noodles.

Egg Noodles (page 52)*
Spinach Noodles (page 53)**
1 tablespoon margarine or butter
1½ cups sliced fresh mushrooms (about 4 ounces)
4 ounces fully cooked smoked ham, cut into 1×¼-inch strips
2 tablespoons chopped fresh parsley
2 tablespoons chopped onion
¼ cup brandy or chicken broth
1 cup whipping (heavy) cream
¼ teaspoon salt
¼ teaspoon pepper
4 quarts water
½ cup freshly grated Parmesan cheese
Freshly ground pepper

Prepare dough for Egg Noodles and Spinach Noodles; cut each into fettuccine as directed. Remove two-thirds of each fettuccine and store for another use.

Melt margarine in 10-inch skillet over medium-high heat. Cook mushrooms, ham, parsley and onion in margarine, stirring occasionally, until mushrooms are tender. Stir in brandy. Cook uncovered until liquid is evaporated. Stir in whipping cream, salt and pepper. Heat to boiling; reduce heat. Simmer uncovered about 15 minutes, stirring frequently, until thickened.

Heat water to boiling in 6- to 8-quart saucepan; add fettuccine. Boil uncovered 2 to 4 minutes, stirring occasionally, until *al dente* (tender but firm). Begin testing for doneness when fettuccine rises to surface of water. Drain fettuccine. Do not rinse. Mix fettuccine and sauce. Sprinkle with cheese. Serve with pepper. *4 servings.*

* 8 ounces fresh or dried fettuccine can be substituted for the Egg Noodles. Cook as directed on package.

** 8 ounces fresh or dried spinach fettuccine can be substituted for the Spinach Noodles. Cook as directed on package.

Nutrition Information Per Serving

1 serving		Percent of U.S. RDA	
Calories	590	Vitamin A	36%
Protein, g	25	Vitamin C	10%
Carbohydrate, g	54	Calcium	26%
Fat, g	32	Iron	26%
Cholesterol, mg	260		
Sodium, mg	900		

Pasta with Three Cheeses

2 tablespoons margarine or butter
2 tablespoons all-purpose flour
1/2 teaspoon salt
1/8 teaspoon pepper
2 cups milk
1 cup shredded Fontina or mozzarella
  cheese (4 ounces)
1 cup shredded Gruyère or Swiss cheese
  (4 ounces)
1/2 cup grated Parmesan cheese
6 cups uncooked egg noodles (10 ounces)
3 tablespoons dry bread crumbs
1 tablespoon margarine or butter

Melt 2 tablespoons margarine in 2-quart saucepan over low heat. Stir in flour, salt and pepper until blended. Cook, stirring constantly, until smooth and bubbly; remove from heat. Gradually stir in milk. Heat to boiling, stirring constantly. Boil and stir 1 minute. Stir in cheeses; keep warm over low heat.

Heat oven to 350°. Cook noodles as directed on package; drain. Alternate layers of noodles and cheese mixture, ending with noodles, in ungreased 2-quart casserole. Heat bread crumbs and 1 tablespoon margarine over medium heat, stirring frequently, until crumbs are toasted; sprinkle over top. Bake uncovered about 20 minutes or until bubbly. *8 servings.*

Nutrition Information Per Serving

1 serving		Percent of U.S. RDA	
Calories	315	Vitamin A	14%
Protein, g	17	Vitamin C	*
Carbohydrate, g	30	Calcium	38%
Fat, g	15	Iron	10%
Cholesterol, mg	60		
Sodium, mg	440		

Pasta Primavera

We used prepared Alfredo sauce to make this a quick dinner perfect for the end of a busy day.

8 ounces uncooked fettuccine or linguine
1 tablespoon olive or vegetable oil
1 cup broccoli flowerets
1 cup cauliflowerets
2 medium carrots, thinly sliced (about
  1 cup)
1 cup frozen green peas, rinsed to
  separate
1 small onion, chopped (about 1/4 cup)
1 container (10 ounces) refrigerated
  Alfredo sauce
1 tablespoon grated Parmesan cheese

Cook fettuccine as directed on package; drain. Heat oil in 12-inch skillet over medium-high heat. Cook broccoli flowerets, cauliflowerets, carrots, peas and onion in oil 6 to 8 minutes stirring frequently, until vegetables are crisp-tender. Stir in Alfredo sauce; cook until hot. Stir in fettuccine; heat through. Sprinkle with cheese. *4 servings.*

Nutrition Information Per Serving

1 serving		Percent of U.S. RDA	
Calories	450	Vitamin A	60%
Protein, g	17	Vitamin C	32%
Carbohydrate, g	69	Calcium	12%
Fat, g	14	Iron	18%
Cholesterol, mg	20		
Sodium, mg	850		

Savory Fusilli

¹/₄ cup olive or vegetable oil
1 tablespoon capers
3 cloves garlic, finely chopped
*2 cans (28 ounces each) whole Italian-
    style tomatoes, drained and chopped*
*1 small red jalapeño chili, seeded and
    chopped*
*¹/₂ cup sliced imported Kalamata or ripe
    olives*
¹/₂ cup sliced pimiento-stuffed olives
*1 tablespoon chopped fresh or 1 teaspoon
    dried oregano leaves*
*1 tablespoon chopped fresh or 1 teaspoon
    dried basil leaves*
*1 package (16 ounces) long fusilli or
    rotini pasta*
Freshly ground pepper

Heat oil in 10-inch skillet over medium-high
heat. Cook capers and garlic in oil, stirring frequently, until garlic is soft. Stir in tomatoes and
chili. Heat to boiling; reduce heat. Cover and
simmer 20 minutes, stirring occasionally. Stir in
olives, oregano and basil. Cover and cook
10 minutes.

Meanwhile, cook pasta as directed on package;
drain. Mix pasta and tomato mixture. Serve with
pepper. *6 servings.*

Nutrition Information Per Serving

1 serving		Percent of U.S. RDA	
Calories	445	Vitamin A	24%
Protein, g	13	Vitamin C	46%
Carbohydrate, g	73	Calcium	12%
Fat, g	14	Iron	30%
Cholesterol, mg	0		
Sodium, mg	1100		

Manicotti

**Try undercooking the manicotti shells by a
few minutes—it will help prevent splitting
when you fill them. The shells will cook completely when they are baked.**

*1 package (8 ounces) manicotti pasta
    shells (14 shells)*
*1¹/₂ cups small curd creamed cottage
    cheese*
¹/₄ cup grated Parmesan cheese
¹/₂ teaspoon salt
¹/₂ teaspoon garlic powder
¹/₈ teaspoon dried thyme leaves
2 eggs
1 small onion, chopped (about ¹/₄ cup)
*1 package (10 ounces) frozen chopped
    spinach, thawed and squeezed to drain*
1 can (8 ounces) tomato sauce
*1 cup shredded mozzarella cheese
    (4 ounces)*

Heat oven to 350°. Grease rectangular pan,
13 × 9 × 2 inches. Cook pasta shells as directed
on package; drain. Mix remaining ingredients
except tomato sauce and mozzarella cheese. Fill
pasta shells with spinach mixture. Place in pan.
Pour tomato sauce over shells. Sprinkle with
mozzarella cheese. Cover and bake about
25 minutes or until hot and bubbly. *7 servings.*

Nutrition Information Per Serving

1 serving		Percent of U.S. RDA	
Calories	370	Vitamin A	42%
Protein, g	26	Vitamin C	8%
Carbohydrate, g	46	Calcium	34%
Fat, g	11	Iron	18%
Cholesterol, mg	110		
Sodium, mg	1720		

Savory Fusilli

Ravioli with Bolognese Sauce

Egg Noodles (page 52) or Spinach
*   Noodles (page 53)*
Bolognese Sauce (page 81)
1 cup chopped fresh spinach
1 container (15 ounces) ricotta cheese
1/2 teaspoon freshly grated nutmeg
1/4 teaspoon salt
4 quarts water
Freshly grated Parmesan cheese, if
*   desired*

Prepare dough for Egg Noodles as directed; roll and cut into 14 rectangles, 12 × 4 inches. (Cover rectangles with plastic wrap until ready to use.) Prepare Bolognese Sauce; keep warm.

Mix spinach, ricotta cheese, nutmeg and salt. Place ten 1-teaspoon mounds of cheese mixture about 1 1/2 inches apart in 2 rows on one rectangle. Moisten dough lightly around mounds with water; top with second rectangle. Press gently around mounds to seal. Cut between mounds into 10 squares, using pastry cutter or knife.* Place in single layer on lightly floured towels; sprinkle lightly with all-purpose flour. Repeat with remaining cheese mixture and rectangles. Let stand uncovered at room temperature 30 minutes. Cook ravioli immediately as directed below, or cover and refrigerate up to 2 days in a single layer on lightly floured towels.

Heat water to boiling in 6- to 8-quart saucepan; add ravioli. Boil uncovered about 6 minutes, stirring occasionally, until *al dente* (tender but firm). Begin testing for doneness when ravioli rise to surface of water. Drain ravioli. Do not rinse. Top ravioli with sauce. Sprinkle with Parmesan cheese. *6 servings.*

*For round ravioli, cut with 2-inch tortelli cutter or round cookie cutter.

Nutrition Information Per Serving

1 serving		Percent of U.S. RDA	
Calories	780	Vitamin A	86%
Protein, g	42	Vitamin C	54%
Carbohydrate, g	75	Calcium	46%
Fat, g	38	Iron	46%
Cholesterol, mg	270		
Sodium, mg	2210		

Pasta Casserole

1 package (16 ounces) mostaccioli pasta
1 jar (26 to 30 ounces) spaghetti sauce
1 container (15 ounces) ricotta cheese
1 package (10 ounces) frozen chopped
*   spinach, thawed and squeezed to drain*
2 green onions, chopped
2 tablespoons sliced pimiento-stuffed
*   olives*
2 tablespoons grated Parmesan cheese
1 tablespoon chopped fresh parsley or
*   1 teaspoon dried parsley flakes*
1/8 teaspoon pepper

Heat oven to 375°. Cook pasta as directed on package; drain. Mix pasta and remaining ingredients. Spoon into ungreased rectangular baking dish, 13 × 9 × 2 inches. Cover and bake about 40 minutes or until hot and bubbly. *8 servings.*

Nutrition Information Per Serving

1 serving		Percent of U.S. RDA	
Calories	370	Vitamin A	30%
Protein, g	16	Vitamin C	6%
Carbohydrate, g	57	Calcium	24%
Fat, g	10	Iron	20%
Cholesterol, mg	15		
Sodium, mg	1010		

Bow-tie Pasta with Favorite Sauce

The enticing blend of seasonings in this sauce made it a favorite of the Savoy royal family, earning it the nickname "favorita"—favorite sauce.

2 tablespoons olive or vegetable oil
1 small red bell pepper, finely chopped (about ¹/₂ cup)
¹/₂ cup chopped fully cooked smoked ham or prosciutto (about 3 ounces)
1 small onion, chopped (about ¹/₄ cup)
2 cloves garlic, finely chopped
1 tablespoon dry white wine or chicken broth
1 can (28 ounces) whole Italian-style tomatoes, undrained
¹/₂ teaspoon pepper
1 package (16 ounces) farfalle (bow-tie) pasta
¹/₄ cup freshly grated Parmesan cheese
1 tablespoon chopped fresh basil leaves

Heat oil in Dutch oven or large saucepan over medium-high heat. Cook pepper, ham, onion and garlic in oil 5 to 7 minutes, stirring occasionally, until onion and pepper are crisp-tender. Stir in wine. Cook uncovered until liquid is evaporated.

Stir in tomatoes and pepper; break up tomatoes. Heat to boiling; reduce heat. Simmer uncovered 45 minutes, stirring occasionally. Cook pasta as directed on package; drain. Mix pasta and sauce. Sprinkle with cheese and basil. *4 servings.*

Nutrition Information Per Serving

1 serving		Percent of U.S. RDA	
Calories	595	Vitamin A	20%
Protein, g	23	Vitamin C	46%
Carbohydrate, g	100	Calcium	14%
Fat, g	14	Iron	34%
Cholesterol, mg	15		
Sodium, mg	1030		

Chicken Jumbo Shells

12 uncooked jumbo pasta shells
1 tablespoon olive or vegetable oil
2 medium tomatoes, seeded and chopped
    (about 1¹/₂ cups)
1 medium stalk celery, thinly sliced (about
    ¹/₂ cup)
1 medium carrot, finely chopped (about
    ¹/₂ cup)
1 clove garlic, finely chopped
1 cup diced cooked chicken
1 tablespoon dry white wine or chicken
    broth
1 container (15 ounces) ricotta cheese
1 cup seasoned croutons
1 teaspoon chopped fresh parsley
¹/₄ teaspoon salt
¹/₄ teaspoon pepper

Cook pasta shells as directed on package; drain. Heat oven to 400°. Grease square pan, 8×8×2 inches. Heat oil in 10-inch skillet over medium-high heat. Cook tomatoes, celery, carrot and garlic in oil 5 to 7 minutes, stirring frequently, until celery and carrot are crisp-tender. Stir in chicken and wine. Cook 5 minutes until wine is evaporated.

Stir remaining ingredients into chicken mixture. Fill cooked shells with chicken mixture. Place filled sides up in pan. Bake uncovered about 10 minutes or until filling is golden brown. *4 servings.*

Nutrition Information Per Serving

1 serving		Percent of U.S. RDA	
Calories	395	Vitamin A	42%
Protein, g	27	Vitamin C	12%
Carbohydrate, g	35	Calcium	32%
Fat, g	17	Iron	14%
Cholesterol, mg	60		
Sodium, mg	520		

Vegetable Jumbo Shells

12 uncooked jumbo pasta shells
1 can (14¹/₂ ounces) vegetable broth
1 medium carrot, finely chopped (about
    ¹/₂ cup)
1 medium potato, peeled and cut into
    ¹/₄-inch pieces (about 1 cup)
1 medium zucchini, cut into ¹/₄-inch pieces
    (about 1 cup)
¹/₂ cup finely chopped broccoli (about
    ¹/₂ cup)
1 tablespoon chopped fresh or 1 teaspoon
    dried basil leaves
2 tablespoons grated Parmesan cheese
2 tablespoons seasoned dry bread crumbs

Cook pasta shells as directed on package; drain. Heat oven to 400°. Heat broth to boiling in 2-quart saucepan. Stir in carrot and potato. Cook 2 to 4 minutes or until crisp-tender. Stir in zucchini and broccoli. Cook 1 minute. Drain vegetables, reserving broth.

Mix vegetables, basil, 1 tablespoon of the cheese and 1 tablespoon of the bread crumbs. Fill cooked shells with vegetable mixture. Pour reserved broth into square baking dish, 8 × 8 × 2 inches. Place filled shells in dish. Mix remaining cheese and bread crumbs; sprinkle over shells. Bake uncovered 10 to 12 minutes or until bread crumbs are golden brown. To serve, spoon broth from dish over shells. *4 servings.*

Nutrition Information Per Serving

1 serving		Percent of U.S. RDA	
Calories	225	Vitamin A	56%
Protein, g	13	Vitamin C	26%
Carbohydrate, g	38	Calcium	8%
Fat, g	4	Iron	14%
Cholesterol, mg	25		
Sodium, mg	410		

Italian Sausage Lasagne

Half-Recipe Egg Noodles (page 52)*
1 tablespoon olive or vegetable oil
4 cloves garlic, finely chopped
³/₄ pound bulk Italian sausage
1 medium onion, chopped (about ¹/₂ cup)
1 medium carrot, chopped (about ¹/₂ cup)
2 cans (28 ounces each) whole Italian-
   style tomatoes, drained
¹/₄ cup packed fresh basil leaves
¹/₄ teaspoon salt
¹/₂ teaspoon pepper
3 cups shredded mozzarella cheese
   (12 ounces)
¹/₂ cup freshly shredded Parmesan cheese

Prepare dough for Egg Noodles as directed; roll and cut into 6 rectangles, 12 × 4 inches. (Cover rectangles with plastic wrap until ready to use.) Heat oil in 10-inch skillet over medium-high heat. Cook garlic, sausage, onion and carrot in oil, stirring occasionally, until sausage is no longer pink; drain.

Place tomatoes and basil in food processor or blender. Cover and process until smooth. Stir tomato mixture, salt and pepper into sausage mixture. Heat to boiling; reduce heat. Simmer uncovered 30 minutes, stirring occasionally.

Heat oven to 375°. Grease rectangular baking dish, 13 × 9 × 2 inches. Mix cheeses. Place 2 rectangles in baking dish; top with half of the sausage mixture and one-third of the cheese mixture. Repeat; top with remaining rectangles and cheese mixture. Cover and bake about 40 minutes or until hot and bubbly. Let stand 15 minutes before cutting. *8 servings.*

* 12 dried lasagne noodles can be substi-tuted for the Half-Recipe Egg Noodles. Cook dried noodles as directed on package. Assemble lasagne as directed above—except substitute 4 cooked dried lasagne noodles for 2 fresh lasagne rectangles.

Nutrition Information Per Serving

1 serving		Percent of U.S. RDA	
Calories	525	Vitamin A	36%
Protein, g	35	Vitamin C	28%
Carbohydrate, g	32	Calcium	56%
Fat, g	30	Iron	20%
Cholesterol, mg	145		
Sodium, mg	1590		

Quick Hot Pasta

Spark your hot pasta dishes with these great ideas to make everyday pasta something special. Cook and drain pasta. Return pasta to same saucepan and combine with the following. Heat until hot if necessary.

- Olive oil, sliced ripe olives, garlic powder, Italian seasoning and grated Parmesan cheese; sprinkle with freshly ground black pepper
- Caesar salad dressing, drained quartered canned artichoke hearts, chopped red bell pepper, cooked cut-up chicken and freshly shredded or grated Parmesan cheese; sprinkle with freshly ground pepper
- Shredded taco-flavored cheese, drained canned corn with red and green peppers, sliced ripe olives and salsa; sprinkle with crushed tortilla or corn chips just before serving
- Purchased peanut sauce, chopped green onion, chopped red bell pepper, chopped fresh cilantro; sprinkle with peanuts just before serving

Two-Sauce Lasagne

This elegant vegetable lasagne showcases both tomato and Alfredo sauces, as well as a pretty layer of fresh basil. It's a great dish for entertaining!

Half-Recipe Egg Noodles (page 52)*
12 uncooked dried lasagne noodles*
1 tablespoon olive or vegetable oil
3 cups thinly sliced fresh mushrooms
    (about 8 ounces)
2 medium carrots, thinly sliced (about
    1 cup)
1 medium onion, chopped (about ¹/₂ cup)
2 cloves garlic, minced
2 cups shredded mozzarella cheese
    (8 ounces)
1 container (15 ounces) ricotta cheese
¹/₂ cup grated Parmesan cheese
1 package (10 ounces) frozen chopped
    spinach, thawed and squeezed to drain
¹/₂ cup chopped fresh or 1¹/₂ teaspoons
    dried basil leaves
1 jar (14 ounces) spaghetti sauce
1 container (10 ounces) refrigerated
    Alfredo sauce
2 tablespoons grated Parmesan cheese

Prepare dough for Egg Noodles as directed; roll and cut into 6 rectangles, 12 × 4 inches. (Cover rectangles with plastic wrap until ready to use.)

Heat oven to 375°. Cook noodles as directed on package; drain. Meanwhile, heat oil in 10-inch skillet over medium-high heat. Cook mushrooms, carrots, onion and garlic in oil 8 to 10 minutes, stirring frequently, until carrots are crisp-tender; drain.

Mix mozzarella, ricotta and ¹/₂ cup Parmesan cheeses. Mix spinach and basil. Spread 1 cup of the spaghetti sauce in ungreased rectangular baking dish, 13 × 9 × 2 inches. Top with 2 rectangles, 1 cup of the cheese mixture, one-third of the vegetable mixture and remaining spaghetti sauce.

Top with 2 rectangles, 1 cup of the cheese mixture, one-third of the vegetable mixture and the spinach mixture. Top with remaining rectangles, cheese mixture and vegetable mixture. Top with Alfredo sauce. Sprinkle with 2 tablespoons Parmesan cheese. Cover and bake 30 minutes. Uncover and bake 15 to 20 minutes longer or until hot and bubbly. Let stand 15 minutes before cutting. *8 servings.*

*12 dried lasagne noodles can be substituted for the Half-Recipe Egg Noodles. Cook dried noodles as directed on package. Assemble lasagne as directed above—except substitute 4 cooked dried lasagne noodles for the 2 fresh lasagne rectangles.

Nutrition Information Per Serving

1 serving		Percent of U.S. RDA	
Calories	525	Vitamin A	84%
Protein, g	25	Vitamin C	*
Carbohydrate, g	41	Calcium	54%
Fat, g	29	Iron	20%
Cholesterol, mg	120		
Sodium, mg	920		

Two-Sauce Lasagne; Spicy Breadsticks (page 29)

Spinach Lasagne

Half-Recipe Egg Noodles (page 52)*
2 tablespoons margarine or butter
3 cups sliced fresh mushrooms (about
 8 ounces)
4 cloves garlic, finely chopped
1 medium onion, thinly sliced
1 medium carrot, thinly sliced (about
 ¹/₂ cup)
3 cups half-and-half
2 tablespoons flour
2 tablespoons pine nuts
1 teaspoon freshly grated nutmeg
¹/₂ teaspoon salt
¹/₂ teaspoon pepper
3 cups shredded mozzarella cheese
 (12 ounces)
1 cup freshly shredded Parmesan cheese
2 packages (10 ounces each) frozen
 chopped spinach, thawed and squeezed
 to drain

Prepare dough for Egg Noodles as directed; roll and cut into 6 rectangles, 12 × 4 inches. (Cover rectangles with plastic wrap until ready to use.)

Melt margarine in 10-inch skillet over medium-high heat. Cook mushrooms, garlic, onion and carrot in margarine 8 to 10 minutes, stirring frequently, until onion and carrot are crisp-tender. Combine half-and-half and flour, blend well. Stir in half-and-half mixture, pine nuts, nutmeg, salt and pepper. Heat to boiling; boil 1 minute or until thickened, stirring constantly.

Heat oven to 375°. Grease rectangular baking dish, 13 × 9 × 2 inches. Mix cheeses. Place 2 rectangles in baking dish; top with half of the spinach, half of the half-and-half mixture and one-third of the cheese mixture. Repeat; top with remaining rectangles and cheese mixture. Cover and bake about 40 minutes or until hot and bubbly. Let stand 15 minutes before cutting. *8 servings.*

*12 dried lasagne noodles can be substituted for the Half-Recipe Egg Noodles. Cook dried noodles as directed on package. Assemble lasagne as directed above—except substitute 4 cooked dried lasagne noodles for 2 fresh lasagne rectangles.

Nutrition Information Per Serving

1 serving		Percent of U.S. RDA	
Calories	615	Vitamin A	84%
Protein, g	26	Vitamin C	8%
Carbohydrate, g	30	Calcium	64%
Fat, g	45	Iron	16%
Cholesterol, mg	210		
Sodium, mg	880		

Lasagne Roll-ups

6 uncooked dried lasagne noodles
6 uncooked dried spinach lasagne noodles
1 pound ground beef
1 large onion, chopped (about 1 cup)
1 jar (14 ounces) spaghetti sauce
1 can (8 ounces) mushroom stems and
 pieces, undrained
1 container (15 ounces) ricotta cheese or
 small curd creamed cottage cheese
 (about 2 cups)
1 package (10 ounces) frozen chopped
 spinach, thawed and squeezed to drain
l cup shredded mozzarella cheese
 (4 ounces)
¹/₄ cup grated Parmesan cheese
1 teaspoon salt
¹/₄ teaspoon pepper
2 cloves garlic, crushed

Heat oven to 350°. Cook noodles as directed on package; drain. Cover noodles with cold water. Cook ground beef and onion in 10-inch skillet, stirring occasionally, until beef is brown; drain. Stir in spaghetti sauce and mushrooms. Heat to boiling. Pour into rectangular baking dish, 11 × 7 × 1¹/₂ inches.

Mix remaining ingredients. Drain noodles. Spread 3 tablespoons of the cheese mixture to edges of 1 noodle. Roll up; cut roll in half to form 2 roll-ups. Place cut sides down in beef mixture. Repeat with remaining noodles and cheese mixture. Cover and bake about 30 minutes or until hot and bubbly. Serve with grated Parmesan cheese, if desired. *8 servings.*

Nutrition Information Per Serving

1 serving		Percent of U.S. RDA	
Calories	405	Vitamin A	30%
Protein, g	27	Vitamin C	6%
Carbohydrate, g	35	Calcium	36%
Fat, g	19	Iron	20%
Cholesterol, mg	70		
Sodium, mg	1120		

Bolognese Sauce

This is the real Bolognese sauce created in Bologna, Italy. Although the sauce is often imitated, this authentic version has a rich and subtle flavor that is a pleasant surprise.

> *2 tablespoons olive or vegetable oil*
> *2 tablespoons margarine or butter*
> *2 medium carrots, finely chopped (about 1 cup)*
> *1 medium onion, chopped (about ¹/₂ cup)*
> *¹/₂ pound bulk Italian sausage*
> *¹/₂ pound lean ground beef*
> *¹/₂ cup dry red wine or beef broth*
> *3 cans (28 ounces each) whole Italian-style tomatoes, drained and chopped*
> *1 teaspoon salt*
> *1 teaspoon dried oregano leaves*
> *¹/₂ teaspoon pepper*

Heat oil and margarine in Dutch oven over medium-high heat until margarine is melted. Cook carrots and onion in oil mixture 8 to 10 minutes, stirring frequently, until carrots and onion are crisp-tender. Stir in sausage and ground beef. Cook over medium heat, stirring occasionally, until sausage and beef are browned and no longer pink; drain.

Stir wine into sausage mixture. Heat to boiling; reduce heat. Simmer uncovered until wine is evaporated. Stir in remaining ingredients. Heat to boiling; reduce heat. Cover and simmer 45 minutes, stirring occasionally. Use sauce immediately, or cover and refrigerate up to 48 hours or freeze up to 2 months. *About 6 cups sauce.*

Nutrition Information Per Serving

1 serving (¹/₂ cup)		Percent of U.S. RDA	
Calories	355	Vitamin A	64%
Protein, g	19	Vitamin C	52%
Carbohydrate, g	22	Calcium	12%
Fat, g	24	Iron	22%
Cholesterol, mg	60		
Sodium, mg	1400		

Sugo Sauce

1 tablespoon olive or vegetable oil
4 cloves garlic, finely chopped
1 small onion, chopped (about ¹/₄ cup)
2 cans (28 ounces each) whole Italian-
* style tomatoes, drained*
2 tablespoons chopped fresh or
* 2 teaspoons dried basil leaves*
2 tablespoons chopped fresh or
* 2 teaspoons dried oregano leaves*
¹/₂ teaspoon salt
¹/₂ teaspoon pepper

Heat oil in 3-quart saucepan over medium-high heat. Cook garlic and onion in oil 5 to 7 minutes, stirring frequently, until onion is crisp-tender. Place tomatoes in food processor or blender. Cover and process until smooth. Stir tomatoes and remaining ingredients into onion mixture. Heat to boiling; reduce heat. Simmer uncovered 45 minutes, stirring occasionally. Use sauce immediately, or cover and refrigerate up to 48 hours or freeze up to 2 months. *About 4¹/₂ cups sauce.*

Nutrition Information Per Serving

1 serving (¹/₂ cup)		Percent of U.S. RDA	
Calories	55	Vitamin A	10%
Protein, g	2	Vitamin C	22%
Carbohydrate, g	9	Calcium	6%
Fat, g	2	Iron	6%
Cholesterol, mg	0		
Sodium, mg	410		

Salsa Rosa

1 tablespoon olive or vegetable oil
1 clove garlic, finely chopped
1 medium onion, chopped (about ¹/₂ cup)
1 tablespoon chopped fresh parsley or
* 1 teaspoon dried parsley flakes*
1 tablespoon chopped fresh or 1 teaspoon
* dried basil leaves*
1 can (28 ounces) whole Italian-style
* tomatoes, drained and chopped*
¹/₂ cup whipping (heavy) cream
¹/₂ teaspoon ground nutmeg
¹/₄ teaspoon salt
¹/₈ teaspoon pepper

Heat oil in 12-inch skillet over medium-high heat. Cook garlic, onion, parsley, basil and tomatoes in oil 10 minutes, stirring occasionally. Stir in remaining ingredients. Cook 15 to 20 minutes, stirring occasionally, until sauce is thickened. Use sauce immediately or cover and refrigerate up to 24 hours. Freezing is not recommended. *About 2 cups sauce.*

Nutrition Information Per Serving

1 serving (¹/₂ cup)		Percent of U.S. RDA	
Calories	165	Vitamin A	20%
Protein, g	3	Vitamin C	28%
Carbohydrate, g	12	Calcium	8%
Fat, g	13	Iron	8%
Cholesterol, mg	35		
Sodium, mg	470		

Egg Noodles with Salsa Rosa

Fresh Tomato Sauce and Noodles

Egg or Spinach Noodles (pages
* 52 and 53)**
Fresh Tomato Sauce (right)
4 quarts water

Prepare dough for Egg or Spinach Noodles; cut into desired width as directed. Remove one-third of the noodles and store for another use. Prepare Fresh Tomato Sauce, reserving 2 cups. Refrigerate or freeze remaining sauce.

Heat water to boiling in 6- to 8-quart saucepan; add noodles. Boil uncovered 2 to 4 minutes, stirring occasionally, until *al dente* (tender but firm). Begin testing for doneness when noodles rise to surface of water. Drain noodles. Do not rinse. Serve sauce over noodles or mix noodles and sauce. *4 servings.*

* 1 package (16 ounces) fresh or dried fettuc-cine or linguine can be substituted for the Egg or Spinach Noodles. Cook as directed on package.

FRESH TOMATO SAUCE

1 can (28 ounces) whole Italian-style
* tomatoes, drained*
2 cloves garlic, finely chopped
1 tablespoon chopped fresh or 1 teaspoon
* dried basil leaves*
1 teaspoon chopped fresh parsley or
* 1 teaspoon dried parsley flakes*
1 teaspoon grated Parmesan cheese
1 teaspoon olive or vegetable oil
¹/₂ teaspoon salt
¹/₂ teaspoon pepper
6 medium tomatoes, diced (about
* 4¹/₂ cups)*
³/₄ cup pitted Kalamata or ripe olives,
* halved*
1 tablespoon capers, if desired

Place all ingredients except tomatoes and capers in food processor or blender. Cover and blend until smooth. Stir in tomatoes, olives and capers. Use sauce immediately or cover and refrigerate up to 48 hours or freeze up to 2 months. *About 4 cups sauce.*

Nutrition Information Per Serving

1 serving (¹/₂ cup)		Percent of U.S. RDA	
Calories	200	Vitamin A	16%
Protein, g	8	Vitamin C	26%
Carbohydrate, g	34	Calcium	6%
Fat, g	5	Iron	18%
Cholesterol, mg	90		
Sodium, mg	490		

Fresh Tomato Sauce and Noodles

Simple Pizza Sauce

*2 cans (28 ounces each) whole Italian-
   style tomatoes, drained*
*1 tablespoon chopped fresh or 1 teaspoon
   dried basil leaves*
*1 tablespoon chopped fresh or 1 teaspoon
   dried oregano leaves*
*1 teaspoon grated Romano or Parmesan
   cheese*
2 teaspoons olive or vegetable oil
¹/₄ teaspoon salt
¹/₄ teaspoon pepper
4 cloves garlic

Place all ingredients in food processor or
blender. Cover and process until smooth. Use
sauce immediately, or cover and refrigerate up
to 48 hours or freeze up to 2 months. *About
3 cups sauce.*

Nutrition Information Per Serving

1 serving (¹/₂ cup)		Percent of U.S. RDA	
Calories	65	Vitamin A	16%
Protein, g	3	Vitamin C	34%
Carbohydrate, g	12	Calcium	8%
Fat, g	2	Iron	10%
Cholesterol, mg	0		
Sodium, mg	530		

Pesto

1 cup chopped fresh basil leaves
¹/₂ cup freshly grated Parmesan cheese
¹/₂ cup pine nuts
¹/₂ cup chopped fresh parsley
¹/₂ cup olive or vegetable oil
1 teaspoon salt
¹/₄ teaspoon pepper
3 cloves garlic

Place all ingredients in food processor or
blender. Cover and process until smooth. Use
sauce immediately or cover and refrigerate up to
5 days or freeze up to 1 month. *About 1¹/₂ cups
sauce.*

Nutrition Information Per Serving

1 serving (1 tablespoon)		Percent of U.S. RDA	
Calories	70	Vitamin A	2%
Protein, g	1	Vitamin C	2%
Carbohydrate, g	1	Calcium	2%
Fat, g	7	Iron	2%
Cholesterol, mg	0		
Sodium, mg	130		

Quick Pasta Sauces

When time is short and appetites are strong, turn to these quick and easy ideas using purchased spaghetti or Alfredo sauce for great-tasting meals in minutes.

Stir-in Ingredients (pick one or more):

- Ground beef or turkey, or bulk or link Italian sausage
- Crispy cooked, crumbled bacon, cooked cut-up roast beef, chicken, ham or turkey
- Canned mushrooms, olives (slices or halves), roasted red peppers or sun-dried tomatoes (sliced or chopped)
- Chopped or sliced fresh vegetables such as bell peppers, carrots, onions, tomatoes, yellow summer squash or zucchini
- Thawed frozen vegetables (any variety)

Directions:

1. If using ground beef, ground turkey or Italian sausage, brown in skillet until no longer pink; drain. If desired, cook bell peppers, carrots, onions, thawed frozen vegetables, tomatoes and zucchini with the meat mixture.

2. If desired, cook bell peppers, carrots, onions, thawed frozen vegetables, tomatoes and zucchini in small amount of olive or vegetable oil until of desired doneness before adding sauce.

3. Stir in sauce; heat until hot, stirring occasionally.

4. If desired, sprinkle with freshly shredded or grated Parmesan cheese or chopped fresh basil or parsley.

Clam Sauce

1 pint shucked fresh small clams, drained and liquid reserved*
1/4 cup olive or vegetable oil
3 cloves garlic, finely chopped
1 can (28 ounces) whole Italian-style tomatoes, drained and chopped
1 small red jalapeño chili, seeded and finely chopped
1 tablespoon chopped fresh parsley
1/2 teaspoon salt

*2 cans (6 1/2 ounces each) minced clams, undrained, can be substituted for the fresh clams.

Chop clams. Heat oil in 10-inch skillet over medium-high heat. Cook garlic in oil, stirring frequently, until soft. Stir in tomatoes and chili. Cook 3 minutes. Stir in clam liquid. Heat to boiling; reduce heat. Simmer uncovered 10 minutes. Stir in clams, parsley and salt. Cover and simmer about 30 minutes, stirring occasionally, until clams are tender. Use sauce immediately or cover and refrigerate up to 48 hours. Freezing is not recommended. *About 2 1/2 cups sauce.*

Nutrition Information Per Serving

1 serving (1/2 cup)		Percent of U.S. RDA	
Calories	195	Vitamin A	26%
Protein, g	13	Vitamin C	44%
Carbohydrate, g	11	Calcium	8%
Fat, g	12	Iron	76%
Cholesterol, mg	30		
Sodium, mg	740		

Mushroom and Brandy Sauce

1 tablespoon butter
4 ounces fresh mushrooms, thinly sliced
   (1¹/₂ cups)
2 tablespoons finely chopped onion
1 clove garlic, finely chopped
¹/₄ cup brandy or chicken broth
2 cups whipping (heavy) cream
¹/₄ teaspoon freshly grated nutmeg
¹/₄ teaspoon pepper

Heat butter in 10-inch skillet over medium-high heat. Cook mushrooms, onion and garlic in butter 5 minutes. Stir in brandy. Heat to boiling. Carefully ignite. Stir in whipping cream, nutmeg and pepper when flames dies out.* Heat to boiling; reduce heat to medium. Simmer uncovered 10 to 20 minutes, stirring frequently, until thickened. *About 2¹/₄ cups sauce. 4 servings.*

 * *To easily extinguish flame, cover with lid.*

Nutrition Information Per Serving

1 serving	(¹/₂ cups)	Percent of U.S. RDA	
Calories	405	Vitamin A	30%
Protein, g	3	Vitamin C	2%
Carbohydrate, g	6	Calcium	8%
Fat, g	40	Iron	2%
Cholesterol, mg	140		
Sodium, mg	60		

4

Chicken, Seafood and Meat

Chicken Marengo (page 96)

Chicken Cacciatore

We used purchased spaghetti sauce to streamline preparation of this savory Italian favorite.

*4 boneless, skinless chicken breast halves
   (about 1 pound)*
2 tablespoons olive or vegetable oil
2 cloves garlic, finely chopped
2 tablespoons finely chopped onion
1 cup sliced fresh mushrooms
*1 medium green bell pepper, chopped
   (about 1 cup)*
¹/₂ cup dry white wine or chicken broth
1 teaspoon red or white wine vinegar
1 jar (14 ounces) spaghetti sauce

Flatten each chicken breast half to ¹/₄-inch thickness between sheets of plastic wrap or waxed paper. Heat oil in 10-inch skillet over medium-high heat. Cook garlic, onion, mushrooms and bell pepper in oil 5 minutes, stirring occasionally.

Add chicken to skillet. Cook about 8 minutes, turning once, until brown. Add wine and vinegar. Cook 3 minutes. Stir in spaghetti sauce.

Cook 10 to 12 minutes or until juice of chicken is no longer pink when centers of thickest pieces are cut. Serve with hot cooked pasta, if desired. *4 servings.*

Nutrition Information Per Serving

1 serving		Percent of U.S. RDA	
Calories	290	Vitamin A	8%
Protein, g	26	Vitamin C	18%
Carbohydrate, g	14	Calcium	6%
Fat, g	14	Iron	12%
Cholesterol, mg	60		
Sodium, mg	810		

Tomatoes

Tomatoes were introduced to Europe after they were discovered in America, but they were used only as ornamental plants. Neapolitans were the first to use tomatoes as a food source, during a famine in the seventeenth century. The region around Naples is where the best pear-shaped tomatoes are grown and canned. They make excellent sauces, having more pulp, more sweetness and less acidity than other tomatoes.

Chicken Cacciatore

Tuscan Chicken Rolls with Pork Stuffing

6 boneless, skinless chicken breast halves
(about 1¹/₂ pounds)
¹/₂ pound ground pork
1 small onion, finely chopped (about
¹/₄ cup)
1 clove garlic, finely chopped
1 egg, beaten
¹/₂ cup soft bread crumbs
¹/₂ teaspoon salt
¹/₄ teaspoon ground savory or crushed
dried savory leaves
¹/₄ teaspoon pepper
2 tablespoons margarine or butter, melted
¹/₂ teaspoon salt
¹/₂ cup dry white wine or chicken broth
¹/₂ cup cold water
2 teaspoons cornstarch
¹/₂ teaspoon chicken bouillon granules
Chopped fresh parsley

Heat oven to 400°. Grease rectangular baking dish, 11×7×1¹/₂ inches. Flatten each chicken breast half to ¹/₄-inch thickness between sheets of plastic wrap or waxed paper. Cook ground pork, onion and garlic in 10-inch skillet over medium heat, stirring occasionally, until pork is no longer pink; drain. Stir in egg, bread crumbs, ¹/₂ teaspoon salt, the savory and pepper.

Place about ¹/₃ cup pork mixture on each chicken breast half to within ¹/₂ inch of edges. Roll up tightly; secure with toothpicks. Place in greased dish. Drizzle rolls with margarine. Sprinkle with ¹/₂ teaspoon salt. Pour wine into dish. Bake uncovered 35 to 40 minutes or until chicken is no longer pink when centers of thickest pieces are cut.

Remove chicken to warm platter; remove toothpicks. Keep chicken warm. Pour liquid from dish into 1-quart saucepan. Stir cold water into cornstarch; pour into liquid in saucepan. Stir in bouillon granules. Heat to boiling over medium heat, stirring constantly. Boil and stir 1 minute. Pour gravy over chicken. Sprinkle with parsley. *6 servings.*

Nutrition Information Per Serving

1 serving		Percent of U.S. RDA	
Calories	320	Vitamin A	6%
Protein, g	35	Vitamin C	*
Carbohydrate, g	9	Calcium	4%
Fat, g	16	Iron	10%
Cholesterol, mg	125		
Sodium, mg	650		

Chicken Piccata

4 boneless, skinless chicken breast halves
  (about 1 pound)
¹/₂ cup all-purpose flour
¹/₄ cup (¹/₂ stick) margarine or butter
2 cloves garlic, finely chopped
1 cup dry white wine or chicken broth
2 tablespoons lemon juice
¹/₄ teaspoon pepper
1 tablespoon capers

Flatten each chicken breast half to ¹/₄-inch thickness between sheets of plastic wrap or waxed paper. Coat chicken with flour. Melt margarine in 12-inch skillet over medium-high heat. Cook chicken and garlic in margarine 4 to 6 minutes, turning chicken once, until juice is no longer pink when centers of thickest pieces are cut. Add wine and lemon juice. Sprinkle chicken with pepper. Heat until hot. Sprinkle with capers. *4 servings.*

Nutrition Information Per Serving

1 serving		Percent of U.S. RDA	
Calories	365	Vitamin A	10%
Protein, g	28	Vitamin C	*
Carbohydrate, g	14	Calcium	2%
Fat, g	15	Iron	12%
Cholesterol, mg	95		
Sodium, mg	140		

Chicken Marsala

4 boneless, skinless chicken breast halves
  (about 1 pound)
¹/₂ cup all-purpose flour
¹/₄ teaspoon salt
¹/₄ teaspoon pepper
2 tablespoons olive or vegetable oil
2 cloves garlic, finely chopped
1 cup sliced fresh mushrooms
¹/₄ cup chopped fresh parsley or
  1 tablespoon dried parsley flakes
¹/₂ cup dry Marsala wine or chicken broth

Flatten each chicken breast half to ¹/₄-inch thickness between sheets of plastic wrap or waxed paper. Mix flour, salt and pepper. Coat chicken with flour mixture; shake off excess flour. Heat oil in 10-inch skillet over medium-high heat. Cook garlic, mushrooms and parsley in oil 5 minutes, stirring frequently.

Add chicken to skillet. Cook about 8 minutes, turning once, until brown. Add wine. Cook 8 to 10 minutes or until juice of chicken is no longer pink when centers of thickest pieces are cut. Serve with hot cooked pasta, if desired. *4 servings.*

Nutrition Information Per Serving

1 serving		Percent of U.S. RDA	
Calories	260	Vitamin A	2%
Protein, g	26	Vitamin C	4%
Carbohydrate, g	14	Calcium	2%
Fat, g	10	Iron	12%
Cholesterol, mg	60		
Sodium, mg	200		

Chicken Marengo

You'll find this is a wonderful dish for enter-taining—we bet you'll find yourself using this easy recipe time and time again.

2 slices bacon, cut into 1-inch pieces
1 medium onion, chopped (about ¹/₂ cup)
2 cloves garlic, finely chopped
1 tablespoon chopped fresh or 1 teaspoon
*   dried rosemary leaves*
4 boneless, skinless chicken breast halves
¹/₂ cup pimiento-stuffed olives
¹/₂ cup dry red wine or chicken broth
1 cup seasoned croutons
1 tablespoon chopped fresh parsley or
*   1 teaspoon dried parsley flakes*

Cook bacon, onion, garlic and rosemary in 10-inch skillet over medium-high heat 6 to 8 minutes, stirring occasionally, until bacon is crisp. Remove bacon with slotted spoon; set aside. Add chicken. Cook 4 to 5 minutes or until chicken is browned. Add olives, wine and bacon. Cover; cook 10 to 12 minutes or until juice of chicken is no longer pink when centers of thickest pieces are cut. Place chicken mixture on serving platter. Sprinkle with croutons and parsley. Serve with hot cooked pasta, if desired. *4 servings.*

Nutrition Information Per Serving

1 serving		Percent of U.S. RDA	
Calories	290	Vitamin A	*
Protein, g	37	Vitamin C	4%
Carbohydrate, g	9	Calcium	4%
Fat, g	10	Iron	12%
Cholesterol, mg	90		
Sodium, mg	690		

Baked Rockfish

¹/₂ cup Pesto (page 86) or purchased pesto
3 tablespoons lemon juice
1 medium carrot, finely chopped (about
*   ¹/₂ cup)*
1 medium leek, chopped
1 drawn rockfish or red snapper (about
*   2 pounds)**

Prepare Pesto. Heat oven to 375°. Grease rectangular baking dish, 13×9×2 inches. Mix sauce, lemon juice, carrot and leek. Place fish in dish. Spread vegetable mixture over fish. Cover and bake about 40 minutes or until fish flakes easily with fork. *4 servings.*

* 2 pounds rockfish or red snapper fillets can be substituted for the drawn fish. Prepare as directed—except increase oven temperature to 450° and bake 15 to 20 minutes or until fish flakes easily with fork.

Nutrition Information Per Serving

1 serving		Percent of U.S. RDA	
Calories	350	Vitamin A	60%
Protein, g	46	Vitamin C	10%
Carbohydrate, g	6	Calcium	12%
Fat, g	16	Iron	8%
Cholesterol, mg	125		
Sodium, mg	460		

Baked Rockfish

Minted Grilled Salmon

If you like to grill fish, you may want to invest in a fish grilling basket. Grill baskets help hold fish together and make turning fish a breeze. They also come in handy for grilling seafood and vegetables.

> *4 small salmon steaks, ³/₄ inch thick*
>   *(about 1¹/₂ pounds)*
> *¹/₂ cup chopped fresh mint leaves*
> *¹/₄ cup olive or vegetable oil*
> *3 tablespoons lemon juice*
> *¹/₂ teaspoon salt*
> *¹/₂ teaspoon pepper*
> *1 clove garlic, finely chopped*
> *1 bay leaf*

Place salmon steaks in ungreased rectangular baking dish, 11×7×1¹/₂ inches. Beat remaining ingredients except bay leaf thoroughly; stir in bay leaf. Drizzle over fish. Cover and refrigerate 1 hour, turning fish over after 30 minutes.

Remove fish from marinade; reserve marinade. Grill fish uncovered about 4 inches from hot coals 10 to 15 minutes, turning over once and brushing with marinade frequently, until fish flakes easily with fork. Heat remaining marinade to rolling boil; remove bay leaf. Serve marinade with fish. *4 servings.*

BROILER DIRECTIONS: Marinate fish as directed. Set oven control to broil. Place fish on rack in broiler pan. Broil with tops about 4 inches from heat about 5 minutes, brushing with marinade frequently, until light brown. Turn carefully; brush with marinade. Broil 4 to 6 minutes longer, brushing with marinade frequently, until fish flakes easily with fork.

Nutrition Information Per Serving

1 serving		Percent of U.S. RDA	
Calories	370	Vitamin A	6%
Protein, g	36	Vitamin C	6%
Carbohydrate, g	2	Calcium	8%
Fat, g	24	Iron	10%
Cholesterol, mg	65		
Sodium, mg	350		

Minted Grilled Salmon

Sole Parmesan

8 thin sole or orange roughy fillets (about
2¹/₂ pounds)
¹/₂ cup all-purpose flour
2 tablespoons margarine or butter
2 green onions, thinly sliced
¹/₂ teaspoon salt
¹/₂ teaspoon pepper
1 cup dry white wine or chicken broth
3 tablespoons lemon juice
¹/₂ cup freshly grated Parmesan cheese

Heat oven to 375°. Coat fish fillets with flour; set aside. Melt margarine in 12-inch ovenproof skillet over medium-low heat. Cook onions in margarine 3 to 5 minutes, stirring occasionally, until crisp-tender. Add fish and cook uncovered 4 minutes; turn fish carefully. Cook 4 minutes longer. Sprinkle with salt and pepper. Pour wine and lemon juice into skillet. Sprinkle with cheese. Bake uncovered 15 minutes or until hot and bubbly. *4 servings.*

Nutrition Information Per Serving

1 serving		Percent of U.S. RDA	
Calories	395	Vitamin A	8%
Protein, g	54	Vitamin C	*
Carbohydrate, g	15	Calcium	22%
Fat, g	13	Iron	10%
Cholesterol, mg	160		
Sodium, mg	750		

Savory Shrimp and Scallops

1 pound fresh or frozen medium shrimp,
peeled and deveined
2 tablespoons olive or vegetable oil
1 clove garlic, finely chopped
1 green onion, chopped
1 medium green bell pepper, diced
1 tablespoon chopped fresh parsley or
1 teaspoon dried parsley flakes
1 pound sea scallops, cut in half
¹/₂ cup dry white wine or chicken broth
1 tablespoon lemon juice
¹/₄ to ¹/₂ teaspoon crushed red pepper

To devein shrimp, make a shallow cut length-wise down back of each shrimp; wash out vein.

Heat oil in 10-inch skillet over medium heat. Cook garlic, onion, bell pepper and parsley in oil about 5 minutes, stirring occasionally, until bell pepper is crisp-tender. Stir in remaining ingredients. Cook 4 to 5 minutes, stirring frequently, until shrimp are pink and scallops are white. Serve with cooked pasta, if desired. *4 servings.*

Nutrition Information Per Serving

1 serving		Percent of U.S. RDA	
Calories	275	Vitamin A	12%
Protein, g	43	Vitamin C	18%
Carbohydrate, g	6	Calcium	16%
Fat, g	9	Iron	34%
Cholesterol, mg	200		
Sodium, mg	490		

Savory Shrimp and Scallops

Savory Tuna

Fresh tuna has a meaty texture that holds up well to all types of preparation. Here, tuna is prepared with pesto and lemon juice for a zesty meal.

> *1 teaspoon olive or vegetable oil*
> *2 green onions, chopped*
> *4 yellowfin tuna or other lean fish fillets,*
>   *³/₄-inch thick (about 1 pound)*
> *¹/₂ cup Pesto (page 86) or purchased pesto*
> *2 tablespoons lemon juice*

Heat oil in 10-inch nonstick skillet over medium heat. Cook onions in oil 2 to 3 minutes, stirring occasionally, until crisp-tender. Add fish fillets, pesto and lemon juice. Heat to boiling; reduce heat. Cover and cook 5 to 10 minutes or until fish flakes easily with fork. *4 servings.*

Nutrition Information Per Serving

1 serving		Percent of U.S. RDA	
Calories	360	Vitamin A	72%
Protein, g	29	Vitamin C	4%
Carbohydrate, g	3	Calcium	14%
Fat, g	26	Iron	12%
Cholesterol, mg	50		
Sodium, mg	160		

Mussels

Mussels are an Italian seaside favorite. To clean mussels, scrub them thoroughly under running water, and then soak in salted water (1 tablespoon salt to 1 gallon water) for 1 hour prior to cooking. Discard any mussels with open or broken shells. Before boiling, remove the mussel "beard"—the anchor that holds the mussel's shell to the rocks—by holding the mussel in one hand and pulling the beard firmly with the other. This ensures that the mussel is tender when cooked.

Venetian Scallops

This dish is best made with sea scallops, which are large, rather than small bay scallops.

1 tablespoon margarine or butter
1 small onion, thinly sliced
1 pound sea scallops, cut in half
$^1/_2$ cup dry white wine or chicken broth
$^1/_2$ cup whipping (heavy) cream
$^1/_4$ teaspoon freshly grated nutmeg
$^1/_4$ cup seasoned dry bread crumbs
$^1/_4$ cup freshly grated Parmesan cheese

Heat oven to 400°. Melt margarine in 10-inch ovenproof skillet over medium-low heat. Cook onion in margarine, stirring occasionally, until tender. Add scallops. Cook 5 minutes. Stir in wine. Cook uncovered until liquid is evaporated. Stir in whipping cream and nutmeg.

Mix bread crumbs and cheese; sprinkle over scallops. Bake uncovered 12 to 15 minutes or until hot and bubbly. *4 servings.*

Nutrition Information Per Serving

1 serving		Percent of U.S. RDA	
Calories	315	Vitamin A	18%
Protein, g	29	Vitamin C	*
Carbohydrate, g	11	Calcium	22%
Fat, g	17	Iron	22%
Cholesterol, mg	90		
Sodium, mg	470		

Pesto

Originally from Genoa, pesto is now used throughout America and Italy. It's a highly versatile sauce made with basil that adds fresh, pungent flavor to pasta, vegetables, *bruschetta* (toasted bread) and salads. Variations on pesto use combinations of other herbs, including parsley and mint, and other nuts (such as walnuts), but the classic recipe found on page 86 is favored over all. When you find fresh basil, be sure to make extra batches of pesto. You can freeze it for later use (don't add the cheese until you thaw the pesto), so that you can enjoy a taste of summer all year long.

Grilled Meatball Kabobs

We suggest using flat metal skewers, rather than round ones, as they help prevent the food from rolling when you're turning the kabobs.

> *1 pound ground beef, pork and veal*
> *   mixture*
> *1 tablespoon chopped fresh parsley*
> *1 tablespoon chopped fresh basil leaves*
> *1 teaspoon salt*
> *¹/₄ teaspoon pepper*
> *1 small onion, finely chopped (about*
> *   ¹/₄ cup)*
> *2 cloves garlic, finely chopped*
> *1 egg*
> *2 large bell peppers, cut into 1-inch*
> *   squares*
> *¹/₄ cup Italian dressing*

Mix all ingredients except bell pepper. Shape mixture into 1-inch balls. Thread meatballs and bell pepper squares alternately on each of four 12-inch metal skewers, leaving space between each. Brush with dressing.

Cover and grill kabobs about 4 inches from hot coals about 10 minutes, turning frequently and brushing with dressing, until meatballs are no longer pink in center. Discard any remaining dressing. *4 servings.*

BROILER DIRECTIONS: Set oven control to broil. Place kabobs on rack in broiler pan. Brush with dressing. Broil with tops about 3 inches from heat 5 minutes. Turn kabobs and brush with dressing. Broil 4 to 5 minutes longer or until meatballs are no longer pink in center. Discard any remaining dressing.

Nutrition Information Per Serving

1 serving		Percent of U.S. RDA	
Calories	245	Vitamin A	4%
Protein, g	21	Vitamin C	20%
Carbohydrate, g	4	Calcium	4%
Fat, g	16	Iron	10%
Cholesterol, mg	125		
Sodium, mg	610		

Grilled Meatball Kabobs

Beef Roast with Parmesan and Cream

This roast beef is rich and delicious! Try serving it with a crisp green salad, crusty rolls and a simply prepared vegetable.

>*2- to 3-pound beef rolled rump roast*
>*1/2 teaspoon pepper*
>*2 ounces Parmesan cheese, cut into*
>   *2 × 1/4 × 1/4-inch strips*
>*2 tablespoons margarine or butter*
>*2 tablespoons olive or vegetable oil*
>*1/2 cup dry red wine or beef broth*
>*2 cups whipping (heavy) cream*
>*Salt and freshly ground pepper to taste*
>*1/2 cup freshly grated Parmesan cheese*

Sprinkle beef roast with 1/2 teaspoon pepper. Make small, deep cuts in all sides of beef with sharp knife. Insert 1 cheese strip completely in each cut. Heat margarine and oil in Dutch oven over medium-high heat until margarine is melted. Cook beef in margarine mixture, turning occasionally, until brown. Add wine. Cook until wine is evaporated.

Insert meat thermometer so that the tip is in center of thickest part of beef and does not touch fat. Pour 2/3 cup of the whipping cream over beef; reduce heat. Cover and cook to desired degree of doneness: 135°F for rare, 23 to 25 minutes per pound; 155°F for medium, 27 to 30 minutes per pound, adding one-third of the remaining whipping cream every 20 minutes.

Sprinkle with salt and pepper. Place beef on warm platter; keep warm. Skim fat from drippings in Dutch oven. Stir grated cheese into drippings. Heat to boiling over medium heat, stirring constantly. Cut beef into thin slices. Serve with sauce. *10 servings.*

Nutrition Information Per Serving

1 serving		Percent of U.S. RDA	
Calories	440	Vitamin A	18%
Protein, g	31	Vitamin C	*
Carbohydrate, g	2	Calcium	18%
Fat, g	34	Iron	14%
Cholesterol, mg	150		
Sodium, mg	350		

Jump-in-the-Mouth Veal

In Italy, this is called "saltimbocca," which translates as "jump in the mouth." The name is a whimsical description of how the combination of flavors springs to life when you taste this dish.

8 small slices veal, ¹/₄-inch thick (about 1¹/₂ pounds)
¹/₂ cup all-purpose flour
8 thin slices fully cooked smoked ham or prosciutto
8 thin slices (1 ounce each) mozzarella cheese
8 fresh sage leaves
¹/₄ cup (¹/₂ stick) margarine or butter
¹/₂ cup dry white wine or chicken broth
¹/₂ teaspoon salt
¹/₄ teaspoon pepper

Pound each slice veal to tenderize. Coat veal with flour. Layer 1 slice each of ham and cheese and 1 sage leaf on each piece of veal. Roll up; secure with toothpick.

Melt margarine in 10-inch skillet over medium heat. Cook veal rolls in margarine, turning occasionally, until brown. Add wine; sprinkle rolls with salt and pepper. Cover and cook over medium-high heat 4 minutes or until veal is no longer pink. *8 servings.*

Nutrition Information Per Serving

1 serving		Percent of U.S. RDA	
Calories	320	Vitamin A	6%
Protein, g	33	Vitamin C	*
Carbohydrate, g	7	Calcium	12%
Fat, g	18	Iron	10%
Cholesterol, mg	135		
Sodium, mg	590		

Veal Piccata

The term "piccata" is a variant of "piccante," or spicy. Thinly sliced veal is covered in a wonderfully spicy, tangy sauce of wine and capers—serve immediately from the skillet to the table.

8 small slices veal, ¹/₄-inch thick (about 1¹/₂ pounds)
¹/₂ cup all-purpose flour
¹/₄ cup (¹/₂ stick) margarine or butter
2 cloves garlic, finely chopped
1 tablespoon capers
¹/₂ cup dry Marsala, dry red wine or beef broth
¹/₂ teaspoon salt
¹/₄ teaspoon pepper

Pound each veal slice to tenderize. Coat veal with flour. Melt margarine in 10-inch skillet over medium-high heat. Cook garlic in margarine, stirring frequently, until soft. Add veal. Cook, turning once, until brown. Add capers and wine. Sprinkle veal with salt and pepper.

Cook uncovered over low heat until wine is evaporated, and veal is no longer pink. Place veal on warm platter; pour any remaining drippings from skillet over veal. *4 servings.*

Nutrition Information Per Serving

1 serving		Percent of U.S. RDA	
Calories	435	Vitamin A	8%
Protein, g	46	Vitamin C	*
Carbohydrate, g	13	Calcium	6%
Fat, g	22	Iron	16%
Cholesterol, mg	220		
Sodium, mg	500		

Veal Parmesan

If you prefer, substitute turkey slices for the veal.

4 veal cutlets (about 4 ounces each) or
 1-pound veal round steak, ¹/₂-inch thick
¹/₂ cup dry bread crumbs
¹/₄ cup grated Parmesan cheese
¹/₂ teaspoon salt
¹/₈ teaspoon pepper
¹/₈ teaspoon paprika
1 egg
¹/₃ cup olive or vegetable oil
3 tablespoons water
1 can (8 ounces) tomato sauce
¹/₂ teaspoon dried oregano leaves, if
 desired

If using veal round steak, cut into 4 servings. Flatten veal to ¹/₄-inch thickness between sheets of plastic wrap or waxed paper. Mix bread crumbs, cheese, salt, pepper and paprika. Beat egg slightly. Dip veal into egg; coat with bread crumb mixture.

Heat oil in 10-inch skillet over medium-high heat. Cook veal in oil about 6 minutes, until brown on both sides, turning once. Reduce heat; add water.

Cover and simmer 30 to 40 minutes or until veal is tender. (If necessary, add small amount of water.)

Remove veal from skillet; keep warm. Add tomato sauce and oregano to skillet. Heat to boiling, stirring occasionally. Serve over veal. *4 servings.*

Nutrition Information Per Serving

1 serving		Percent of U.S. RDA	
Calories	400	Vitamin A	8%
Protein, g	23	Vitamin C	*
Carbohydrate, g	14	Calcium	10%
Fat, g	28	Iron	10%
Cholesterol, mg	125		
Sodium, mg	870		

Grilled Meat and Vegetable Kabobs

¹/₄ cup Pesto (page 86) or purchased pesto
³/₄-pound lamb boneless shoulder, cut into
*   1-inch cubes*
³/₄-pound beef or veal tenderloin, cut into
*   1-inch cubes*
¹/₂ cup dry white wine or chicken broth
3 tablespoons lemon juice
8 ounces fresh medium mushrooms, stems
*   removed*
1 medium red bell pepper, cut into 1-inch
*   pieces*
1 medium green bell pepper, cut into
*   1-inch pieces*
1 medium yellow bell pepper, cut into
*   1-inch pieces*
16 fresh sage leaves
2 leeks, cut into 1-inch pieces
8 cherry tomatoes

Prepare Pesto. Place lamb and beef in glass or plastic bowl. Mix pesto, wine and lemon juice; pour over meat. Cover and refrigerate 1 hour.

Remove meat from marinade; reserve marinade. Thread meat, mushrooms, bell peppers, sage leaves and leeks alternately on each of eight 9-inch metal skewers, leaving space between each. Top each with tomato.

Cover and grill kabobs about 4 inches from hot coals about 16 minutes, turning once and brushing with marinade occasionally, until meat is done. Discard any remaining marinade.
6 servings.

BROILER DIRECTIONS: Set oven control to broil. Place kabobs on rack in broiler pan. Broil with tops about 3 inches from heat 5 minutes. Turn kabobs; brush with marinade. Broil 5 minutes longer. Turn kabobs again; brush with marinade. Broil about 5 minutes longer or until meat is done. Discard any remaining marinade.

Nutrition Information Per Serving

1 serving		Percent of U.S. RDA	
Calories	430	Vitamin A	28%
Protein, g	29	Vitamin C	50%
Carbohydrate, g	9	Calcium	6%
Fat, g	31	Iron	20%
Cholesterol, mg	100		
Sodium, mg	170		

Peppered Pork Chops

*1 tablespoon whole black peppercorns,
  coarsely crushed*
6 pork loin chops, ¹/₂-inch thick
1 tablespoon margarine or butter
1 tablespoon olive or vegetable oil
4 cloves garlic, cut in half
1 cup sliced fresh mushrooms
¹/₂ teaspoon salt
*¹/₂ cup dry Marsala, dry red wine or beef
  broth*

Sprinkle half the crushed peppercorns over one side of pork chops; gently press into pork. Turn pork; repeat with remaining peppercorns.

Heat margarine and oil in 12-inch nonstick skillet over medium-high heat until margarine is melted. Cook garlic in margarine mixture, stirring frequently, until golden. Add pork; cook uncovered 5 minutes. Turn pork. Add mushrooms, salt and wine; reduce heat. Cover and simmer about 5 minutes longer or until pork is tender and no longer pink in center. *6 servings.*

Nutrition Information Per Serving

1 serving		Percent of U.S. RDA	
Calories	330	Vitamin A	2%
Protein, g	21	Vitamin C	*
Carbohydrate, g	3	Calcium	2%
Fat, g	26	Iron	8%
Cholesterol, mg	75		
Sodium, mg	230		

Pork Roast with Rosemary

2¹/₂- to 3-pound pork loin roast
*2 tablespoons chopped fresh rosemary
  leaves*
4 cloves garlic, finely chopped
1 teaspoon salt
¹/₂ teaspoon pepper
1 tablespoon margarine or butter
1 small onion, chopped (about ¹/₄ cup)
2 tablespoons olive or vegetable oil

Heat oven to 350°. Trim fat from pork roast. Mix rosemary and garlic. Make 8 to 10 deep cuts about 2 inches apart in pork with sharp knife. Insert small amounts of garlic mixture in cuts. Sprinkle pork with salt and pepper.

Melt margarine in shallow roasting pan in oven; sprinkle with onion. Place pork in pan; drizzle with oil. Insert meat thermometer so that tip is in center of thickest part of pork and does not touch fat. Roast uncovered 1³/₄ to 2 hours or until thermometer reads 160°. Let stand 15 minutes before slicing. *12 servings.*

Nutrition Information Per Serving

1 serving		Percent of U.S. RDA	
Calories	340	Vitamin A	*
Protein, g	23	Vitamin C	*
Carbohydrate, g	1	Calcium	2%
Fat, g	27	Iron	6%
Cholesterol, mg	80		
Sodium, mg	230		

Pork Roast with Rosemary

Grilled Lamb Chops with Mint

Lamb is very popular in the south of Italy as its drier climate is more suited to raising sheep and goats, whereas beef and pork are common in Northern Italy. Mint adds wonderful freshness to these lamb chops.

> *8 lamb loin chops (about 1¼ pounds),*
>   *½-inch thick*
> *½ cup chopped fresh mint leaves*
> *½ cup wine vinegar*
> *¼ cup olive or vegetable oil*
> *1 tablespoon sugar*
> *½ teaspoon salt*
> *¼ teaspoon pepper*

Place lamb chops in rectangular glass baking dish, 11×7×1½ inches. Place ¼ cup of the mint and the remaining ingredients in food processor or blender. Cover and process until smooth; pour over lamb. Cover and refrigerate 1 hour.

Remove lamb from marinade; reserve marinade. Toss remaining mint onto hot coals. Cover and grill lamb about 4 to 6 inches from hot coals about 10 minutes, turning once and brushing with marinade occasionally, or until lamb is medium doneness (160°F). Discard any remaining marinade. *4 servings.*

BROILED LAMP CHOPS WITH MINT: Decrease mint to ¼ cup. Marinate lamb as directed. Set oven control to broil. Place lamb on rack in broiler pan. Broil with tops about 2 inches from heat about 6 minutes or until brown. Turn lamb. Broil 5 to 6 minutes longer or until lamb is medium doneness (160°F). Discard any remaining marinade.

Nutrition Information Per Serving

1 serving		Percent of U.S. RDA	
Calories	345	Vitamin A	2%
Protein, g	20	Vitamin C	*
Carbohydrate, g	3	Calcium	2%
Fat, g	28	Iron	12%
Cholesterol, mg	80		
Sodium, mg	190		

Grilled Lamb Chops with Mint; Zucchini with Fresh Herbs (page 133)

5

Risotto, Polenta and More

Risotto with Zucchini and Peppers (page 116)

Four-Cheese Risotto

This creamy cheese risotto is excellent served with grilled steak or pork.

2 tablespoons olive or vegetable oil
1 medium onion, chopped (about ¹/₂ cup)
1 cup uncooked Arborio or regular long grain rice
1 tablespoon dry white wine or chicken broth
3¹/₂ cups chicken broth
¹/₂ cup ricotta cheese
¹/₄ cup shredded mozzarella cheese (1 ounce)
¹/₄ cup crumbled blue cheese
¹/₄ cup grated Parmesan cheese
1 tablespoon chopped fresh parsley or 1 teaspoon dried parsley flakes

Heat oil in 3-quart saucepan over medium-high heat. Cook onion in oil 4 to 5 minutes, stirring frequently, until crisp-tender. Stir in rice. Cook 3 minutes, stirring frequently. Add wine. Cook until liquid is evaporated.

Pour ¹/₂ cup broth over rice mixture. Cook uncovered, stirring occasionally, until liquid is absorbed. Continue cooking 15 to 20 minutes, adding broth ¹/₂ cup at a time and stirring occasionally, until rice is tender and creamy. Stir in cheeses. Sprinkle with parsley. *4 to 6 servings.*

Nutrition Information Per Serving

1 serving		Percent of U.S. RDA	
Calories	390	Vitamin A	6%
Protein, g	18	Vitamin C	2%
Carbohydrate, g	45	Calcium	28%
Fat, g	16	Iron	14%
Cholesterol, mg	25		
Sodium, mg	940		

Risotto with Zucchini and Peppers

1 tablespoon margarine or butter
2 medium zucchini, cut into julienne strips
2 medium bell peppers, cut into strips
1 medium onion, thinly sliced
1 tablespoon olive or vegetable oil
2 cups uncooked Arborio or regular long grain rice
3¹/₃ cups chicken broth
1 cup half-and-half
¹/₃ cup dry white wine or chicken broth
¹/₄ teaspoon pepper
2 tablespoons freshly grated Parmesan cheese

Heat margarine in 12-inch skillet or Dutch oven over medium-high heat until margarine is melted. Cook zucchini, peppers and onion in margarine 5 to 7 minutes, until crisp-tender, stirring occasionally. Remove from skillet; set aside. Heat oil in same skillet over medium-high heat; stir in rice. Cook uncovered, stirring frequently, until rice begins to brown. Reduce heat to medium.

Mix broth, half-and-half and pepper; pour ¹/₂ cup broth mixture over rice mixture. Cook uncovered, stirring occasionally, until liquid is absorbed. Continue cooking 15 to 20 minutes, adding broth ¹/₂ cup at a time and stirring occasionally, until rice is tender and creamy. Stir in reserved zucchini mixture. Sprinkle with cheese. *6 servings.*

Nutrition Information Per Serving

1 serving		Percent of U.S. RDA	
Calories	385	Vitamin A	8%
Protein, g	11	Vitamin C	10%
Carbohydrate, g	61	Calcium	10%
Fat, g	11	Iron	16%
Cholesterol, mg	20		
Sodium, mg	500		

Gorgonzola Risotto

Gorgonzola and walnuts are a delicious pair, and a generous sprinkling of toasted walnuts adds a wonderful finishing touch to this risotto.

> 2 tablespoons margarine or butter
> 1 medium onion, thinly sliced
> 1 medium carrot, thinly sliced (about
>   1/2 cup)
> 2 cups uncooked Arborio rice or regular
>   long grain rice
> 3 1/3 cups milk
> 1 1/3 cups half-and-half
> 1/3 cup crumbled Gorgonzola or blue
>   cheese
> 1 package (3 ounces) cream cheese, cut
>   into cubes
> 1/4 teaspoon pepper

Melt margarine in 12-inch skillet or Dutch oven over medium-high heat. Cook onion and carrot in margarine 5 to 7 minutes, stirring occasionally, until crisp-tender. Reduce heat to medium; stir in rice. Cook uncovered, stirring frequently, until rice begins to brown.

Mix milk and half-and-half; pour 1/2 cup milk mixture over rice mixture. Cook uncovered, stirring occasionally, until liquid is absorbed. Continue cooking 15 to 20 minutes, adding milk 1/2 cup at a time and stirring occasionally, until rice is tender and creamy. Stir in cheeses and pepper. Cook about 5 minutes, stirring frequently, until cheeses are melted. *8 servings.*

Nutrition Information Per Serving

1 serving		Percent of U.S. RDA	
Calories	375	Vitamin A	36%
Protein, g	11	Vitamin C	*
Carbohydrate, g	49	Calcium	22%
Fat, g	15	Iron	10%
Cholesterol, mg	45		
Sodium, mg	200		

Risotto with Shrimp

Just add a fresh green salad and crusty rolls for a complete meal.

> 1 pound raw medium shrimp in shells,
>   peeled and deveined
> 2 tablespoons margarine or butter
> 1 medium onion, thinly sliced
> 1/2 cup dry white wine or chicken broth
> 1 1/2 cups uncooked Arborio or regular
>   long grain rice
> 2 cups chicken broth
> 1 cup water
> 1/4 cup freshly grated Parmesan cheese
> Freshly ground pepper

To devein shrimp, make a shallow cut lengthwise down back of each shrimp; wash out vein. Melt margarine in 12-inch skillet or Dutch oven over medium-high heat. Cook onion in margarine 8 to 10 minutes, stirring frequently, until tender. Reduce heat to medium; add shrimp. Cook uncovered about 8 minutes, turning once, until shrimp are pink. Remove shrimp from skillet; keep warm.

Add wine to skillet. Cook until liquid is evaporated. Stir in rice. Cook uncovered over medium heat, stirring frequently, until rice is light brown. Mix broth and water; pour 1/2 cup broth mixture over rice. Continue cooking 15 to 20 minutes, adding broth 1/2 cup at a time and stirring occasionally, until rice is tender and creamy. Stir in shrimp. Sprinkle with cheese and pepper. *6 servings.*

Nutrition Information Per Serving

1 serving		Percent of U.S. RDA	
Calories	280	Vitamin A	6%
Protein, g	15	Vitamin C	*
Carbohydrate, g	42	Calcium	10%
Fat, g	6	Iron	16%
Cholesterol, mg	85		
Sodium, mg	450		

Chicken Risotto

Saffron gives this risotto a lovely yellow color. If saffron is not available, you can substitute turmeric for the same pretty shade.

2 tablespoons olive or vegetable oil
⅓ cup chopped green onions
1 medium carrot, thinly sliced (about ½ cup)
2 cloves garlic, finely chopped
1 cup uncooked Arborio or regular long grain rice
3½ cups chicken broth
1 tablespoon chopped fresh parsley
⅛ teaspoon saffron threads, crushed, or ground turmeric
2 cups cut-up cooked chicken

Heat oil in 3-quart saucepan over medium-high heat. Cook onions, carrot and garlic in oil about 4 to 5 minutes, stirring frequently, until carrots are crisp-tender. Stir in rice. Cook, stirring frequently, until rice begins to brown.

Pour ½ cup broth, parsley and saffron over rice. Cook uncovered, stirring occasionally, until liquid is absorbed. Continue cooking 15 to 20 minutes, adding broth ½ cup at a time and stirring occasionally, until rice is tender and creamy. Stir in chicken; heat through. *6 servings.*

Nutrition Information Per Serving

1 serving		Percent of U.S. RDA	
Calories	270	Vitamin A	18%
Protein, g	19	Vitamin C	2%
Carbohydrate, g	29	Calcium	2%
Fat, g	9	Iron	12%
Cholesterol, mg	40		
Sodium, mg	280		

Risotto

Northern Italians favor rice and cornmeal over pasta, using many variations of them. The classic rice dish is risotto, in which Arborio rice is cooked with broth and an almost endless variety of ingredients—such as meats and vegetables—to create a rice that is tender and creamy, yet retains some firmness. The trick is in the slow cooking of the rice, judicious stirring and regulating the amount of liquid added. It's easy to learn to prepare a classic risotto such as Gorgonzola Risotto (page 117).

Chicken Risotto

Polenta with Cheese

Serve this satisfying polenta with grilled chicken.

1 cup yellow cornmeal
³/₄ cup water
3¹/₄ cups boiling water
2 teaspoons salt
1 tablespoon margarine or butter
1 cup grated Parmesan cheese
¹/₃ cup shredded Swiss cheese

Heat oven to 350°. Grease 1¹/₂-quart casserole. Mix cornmeal and ³/₄ cup water in 2-quart saucepan. Stir in 3¹/₄ cups boiling water and the salt. Cook over medium-high heat, stirring constantly, until mixture thickens and boils; reduce heat. Cover and simmer 10 minutes, stirring occasionally; remove from heat. Stir until smooth.

Spread one-third of the polenta in casserole; dot with one-third of the margarine and sprinkle with ¹/₃ cup of the Parmesan cheese. Repeat twice. Sprinkle with Swiss cheese. Bake uncovered 15 to 20 minutes or until hot and bubbly. *6 servings.*

Nutrition Information Per Serving

1 serving		Percent of U.S. RDA	
Calories	185	Vitamin A	6%
Protein, g	9	Vitamin C	*
Carbohydrate, g	19	Calcium	24%
Fat, g	8	Iron	6%
Cholesterol, mg	15		
Sodium, mg	1000		

Polenta with Sausage

Polenta—what many people know as cornmeal mush—has been made for decades, but is just now taking a place of honor in restaurants. You'll love this at-home version, sparked with sausage and Parmesan cheese.

Sugo Sauce (page 82) or 4¹/₂ cups purchased spaghetti sauce
4 cups water
1¹/₂ teaspoons salt
1¹/₂ cups yellow cornmeal
1 small onion, thinly sliced
³/₄ pound bulk Italian sausage
¹/₂ cup freshly grated Parmesan cheese

Prepare Sugo Sauce. Heat water and salt to boiling in Dutch oven. Gradually add cornmeal, stirring constantly. Reduce heat to low. Cook uncovered about 30 minutes, stirring frequently, until mixture is very thick and smooth. Spread in ungreased square baking dish, 9×9×2 inches. Cover and keep warm.

Cook onion and sausage in 10-inch skillet over medium-high heat, until sausage is no longer pink; drain. Stir in Sugo Sauce. Heat to boiling; reduce heat. Simmer uncovered 20 minutes, stirring occasionally. Cut polenta into pieces. Spoon sausage mixture over polenta. Sprinkle with cheese. *8 servings.*

Nutrition Information Per Serving

1 serving		Percent of U.S. RDA	
Calories	315	Vitamin A	10%
Protein, g	15	Vitamin C	20%
Carbohydrate, g	30	Calcium	16%
Fat, g	15	Iron	16%
Cholesterol, mg	40		
Sodium, mg	1150		

Polenta with Sausage

Polenta Wedges

2 tablespoons olive or vegetable oil
1 medium onion, finely chopped (about
   ¹/₂ cup)
2 cans (14¹/₂ ounces each) vegetable broth
1 cup yellow cornmeal
¹/₄ teaspoon salt
¹/₈ teaspoon pepper
¹/₄ cup Pesto (page 86) or purchased pesto
¹/₄ cup grated Parmesan cheese

Heat oil in 3-quart saucepan over medium heat. Cook onion in oil 4 to 5 minutes, stirring occasionally, until tender. Stir in broth. Heat to boiling. Gradually stir in cornmeal. Stir in salt and pepper; reduce heat. Cover and simmer 15 to 20 minutes, stirring occasionally, until mixture is thick and smooth.

Grease 10-inch dinner plate or serving platter. Spread polenta over plate; cool 5 minutes. Cut into 4 wedges. Top each wedge with pesto. Sprinkle with cheese. *4 servings.*

Nutrition Information Per Serving

1 serving		Percent of U.S. RDA	
Calories	440	Vitamin A	50%
Protein, g	21	Vitamin C	4%
Carbohydrate, g	42	Calcium	16%
Fat, g	23	Iron	18%
Cholesterol, mg	45		
Sodium, mg	740		

Chicken and Mushroom Polenta

1 tablespoon olive or vegetable oil
1 cup sliced fresh mushrooms
1 medium onion, finely chopped (about
   ¹/₂ cup)
3¹/₂ cups chicken broth
1 cup yellow cornmeal
1 tablespoon chopped fresh parsley or
   1 teaspoon dried parsley flakes
¹/₂ teaspoon dried oregano leaves
¹/₂ teaspoon dried basil leaves
2 cups cut-up cooked chicken

Heat oil in 3-quart saucepan over medium heat. Cook mushrooms and onion in oil 4 to 5 minutes, stirring occasionally, until tender. Stir in broth. Heat to boiling. Gradually stir in cornmeal. Stir in parsley, oregano and basil; reduce heat. Cover and simmer 15 to 20 minutes, stirring occasionally, until liquid is absorbed and mixture is thick and smooth. Stir in chicken; heat through. *4 to 6 servings.*

Nutrition Information Per Serving

1 serving		Percent of U.S. RDA	
Calories	315	Vitamin A	2%
Protein, g	28	Vitamin C	2%
Carbohydrate, g	31	Calcium	4%
Fat, g	10	Iron	18%
Cholesterol, mg	60		
Sodium, mg	710		

Spinach Gnocchi with Nutmeg

Simple ingredients combine for an outstanding first course, or try the gnocchi as a rich, creamy side dish.

1 medium potato
¹/₂ teaspoon salt
1 teaspoon freshly grated nutmeg
1 jumbo egg
1 package (10 ounces) frozen chopped spinach, thawed and squeezed to drain
1 to 1¹/₃ cups all-purpose flour
1 tablespoon margarine or butter
2 green onions, thinly sliced
¹/₂ cup whipping (heavy) cream
¹/₄ teaspoon white pepper
4 quarts water
¹/₄ cup freshly grated Parmesan cheese

Heat potato and enough water to cover to boiling. Cover and boil about 30 minutes or until tender; drain and cool slightly. Peel and mash potato; cool. Stir in salt, nutmeg, egg, spinach and enough of the flour to make a stiff dough. Shape into 1-inch balls.

Melt margarine in 10-inch skillet over medium-high heat. Cook onions in margarine 2 to 4 minutes, stirring occasionally, until crisp-tender. Stir in whipping cream and white pepper. Heat to boiling; reduce heat. Simmer uncovered 5 to 10 minutes or until slightly thickened; keep warm.

Heat water to boiling in 6- to 8-quart saucepan; add half of the gnocchi. After gnocchi rise to surface, boil 4 minutes. Remove with slotted spoon; drain. Repeat with remaining gnocchi. Spoon cream mixture over gnocchi. Sprinkle with cheese. *4 servings.*

Nutrition Information Per Serving

1 serving		Percent of U.S. RDA	
Calories	355	Vitamin A	52%
Protein, g	11	Vitamin C	4%
Carbohydrate, g	37	Calcium	20%
Fat, g	18	Iron	14%
Cholesterol, mg	120		
Sodium, mg	480		

Polenta

Since its introduction to Italy, corn has been a staple in the regions surrounding Venice (Veneto, Lombardy, Piedmont, Emilia and Romagna). Italians have eaten polenta, made from cornmeal, for centuries; it is a favorite substitute for bread or pasta, served hot or cold. When warm, polenta is served with butter or cheese, or such meats as sausage, small game birds and even shellfish. Cold, polenta is just as versatile; it can be baked, fried, grilled or broiled. Try cutting cold polenta into cubes, covering them with tomato sauce and Parmesan cheese and baking in a 375° oven for 20 minutes. Delicious!

Eggplant Parmigiana

When selecting eggplant, look for those that are heavy for their size, with a smooth and shiny skin.

2 medium eggplant (about 1¹/₂ pounds)
¹/₃ cup milk
¹/₂ cup seasoned dry bread crumbs
¹/₂ cup olive or vegetable oil
1 jar (14 ounces) spaghetti sauce
1 tablespoon chopped fresh or 1 teaspoon
  dried basil leaves
¹/₂ cup grated Parmesan cheese
1 cup shredded mozzarella cheese
  (4 ounces)
1 tablespoon chopped fresh parsley or
  1 teaspoon dried parsley flakes

Heat oven to 400°. Peel eggplant; cut crosswise into ¹/₂-inch slices. Dip eggplant slices into milk; coat with bread crumbs. Heat oil in 12-inch nonstick skillet over medium heat. Cook eggplant slices in oil about 2 minutes on each side or until tender and golden brown.

Mix spaghetti sauce and basil; spread ³/₄ cup of the sauce in ungreased rectangular baking dish, 13×9×2 inches. Arrange half the eggplant slices on sauce. Sprinkle with ¹/₄ cup of the Parmesan cheese and ¹/₂ cup of the mozzarella cheese. Top with ¹/₂ cup of the sauce and remaining eggplant slices. Sprinkle with remaining cheeses. Top with remaining sauce. Cover and bake about 20 minutes or until cheese is bubbly. Sprinkle with parsley. *6 servings.*

Nutrition Information Per Serving

1 serving		Percent of U.S. RDA	
Calories	270	Vitamin A	10%
Protein, g	12	Vitamin C	*
Carbohydrate, g	26	Calcium	30%
Fat, g	13	Iron	10%
Cholesterol, mg	20		
Sodium, mg	750		

Parmesan and Romano

Parmesan and Romano are two favorite Italian cheeses used in many dishes. Parmesan comes from the district of Parma in Northern Italy and is usually aged for more than a year before it is sold. Parmesan has a dense texture and flakes easily when grated for topping pasta. It holds its shape when used for baking and is used for pasta, meat and vegetable dishes.

Romano cheese is made from sheep's milk, not cow's milk as is Parmesan. The two types of Romano cheese in Italy are Pecorino Romano, from Rome, and Pecorino Sardo, from the island of Sardinia. Romano has a drier, sharper flavor than Parmesan and is well-suited for pasta served with cured meats such as prosciutto or bacon. It can be added to salads for extra flavor or eaten with bread and a glass of wine. Romano's more pungent flavor is due to the diet of the sheep, which graze in sparse pastures—unlike cows, which graze in the fertile fields of Northern Italy and produce Parmesan.

Eggplant Parmigiana

Sunny Frittata

This recipe takes its name from the bright yellow bell peppers and its cheerful, round sun shape.

> *1 tablespoon olive or vegetable oil*
> *¹/₂ cup sliced fresh mushrooms*
> *1 tablespoon chopped drained sun-dried tomatoes in oil*
> *2 green onions, chopped*
> *1 small yellow bell pepper, chopped (about ¹/₂ cup)*
> *8 eggs*
> *1 tablespoon chopped fresh parsley or 1 teaspoon dried parsley flakes*
> *1 tablespoon chopped fresh or ¹/₂ teaspoon dried basil leaves*
> *1 tablespoon grated Parmesan cheese*
> *¹/₂ teaspoon salt*
> *¹/₄ teaspoon pepper*

Heat oil in 10-inch ovenproof skillet over medium heat. Cook mushrooms, tomatoes, onions and bell pepper in oil 3 minutes, stirring occasionally. Reduce heat to medium-low. Beat remaining ingredients until blended. Pour over vegetable mixture. Cover and cook 9 to 11 minutes or until eggs are set around edge and light brown on bottom.

Set oven control to broil. Broil frittata with top about 5 inches from heat about 3 minutes or until golden brown. *6 servings.*

Nutrition Information Per Serving

1 serving		Percent of U.S. RDA	
Calories	125	Vitamin A	12%
Protein, g	9	Vitamin C	8%
Carbohydrate, g	2	Calcium	4%
Fat, g	9	Iron	6%
Cholesterol, mg	280		
Sodium, mg	280		

Savory Italian Frittata

> *8 eggs*
> *¹/₄ cup diced fully cooked smoked ham or prosciutto (about 2 ounces)*
> *1 tablespoon chopped fresh or ¹/₂ teaspoon dried basil leaves*
> *1 tablespoon chopped fresh or ¹/₂ teaspoon dried sage leaves*
> *1 tablespoon chopped fresh or ¹/₂ teaspoon dried mint leaves*
> *1 tablespoon freshly grated Parmesan cheese*
> *¹/₂ teaspoon salt*
> *¹/₈ teaspoon pepper*
> *1 tablespoon margarine or butter*
> *1 small onion, finely chopped (about ¹/₄ cup)*

Beat all ingredients except margarine and onion thoroughly. Melt margarine in 10-inch nonstick skillet over medium-high heat. Cook onion in margarine 4 to 5 minutes, stirring frequently, until crisp-tender.

Reduce heat to medium-low. Pour egg mixture into skillet. Cover and cook 9 to 11 minutes or until eggs are set around edge and light brown on bottom. *6 servings.*

Nutrition Information Per Serving

1 serving		Percent of U.S. RDA	
Calories	140	Vitamin A	12%
Protein, g	11	Vitamin C	*
Carbohydrate, g	2	Calcium	6%
Fat, g	10	Iron	6%
Cholesterol, mg	300		
Sodium, mg	380		

Savory Italian Frittata

6

Garden Vegetables and Salad

Tortellini Salad (page 137)

Neapolitan Potatoes

Try using the new Yukon gold potatoes in this dish—they have a golden yellow color, even after cooking.

2 pounds potatoes (about 5 medium)
2 medium tomatoes, seeded and chopped
   (about 1¹/₂ cups)
2 cloves garlic, finely chopped
1 cup shredded mozzarella cheese
   (4 ounces)
2 tablespoons olive or vegetable oil
2 tablespoons chopped fresh or 1 teaspoon
   dried basil leaves
¹/₂ teaspoon salt
¹/₄ teaspoon pepper
2 tablespoons chopped green onion

Place potatoes in 2-quart saucepan; add enough water to cover. Heat to boiling; reduce heat. Cook 20 to 25 minutes or until tender; drain and cool slightly. Peel potatoes; cut into 1-inch pieces.

Place potatoes and remaining ingredients in large glass or plastic bowl; toss gently. Cover and refrigerate 1 to 2 hours to blend flavors. *8 servings.*

Nutrition Information Per Serving

1 serving		Percent of U.S. RDA	
Calories	230	Vitamin A	4%
Protein, g	5	Vitamin C	12%
Carbohydrate, g	18	Calcium	10%
Fat, g	16	Iron	2%
Cholesterol, mg	10		
Sodium, mg	210		

Artichoke Hearts with Olives and Potatoes

1 pound small red potatoes, cut in half
¹/₃ cup olive or vegetable oil
1 small onion, thinly sliced
2 packages (9 ounces each) frozen
   artichoke hearts, thawed
¹/₄ cup sliced pitted green olives
2 tablespoons lemon juice
1 tablespoon capers
¹/₂ teaspoon salt
¹/₈ teaspoon pepper
Freshly grated Parmesan cheese, if
   desired

Place potatoes in 3-quart saucepan; add enough water to cover. Heat to boiling; reduce heat. Cover and simmer about 10 minutes or until tender; drain.

Heat oil in 12-inch skillet over medium-high heat. Cook onion in oil 5 to 7 minutes, stirring frequently, until tender. Reduce heat to medium. Stir in potatoes and remaining ingredients except cheese. Cook uncovered about 5 minutes, stirring frequently, until hot. Sprinkle with cheese. *4 servings.*

Nutrition Information Per Serving

1 serving		Percent of U.S. RDA	
Calories	330	Vitamin A	2%
Protein, g	7	Vitamin C	22%
Carbohydrate, g	40	Calcium	8%
Fat, g	19	Iron	18%
Cholesterol, mg	0		
Sodium, mg	610		

Neapolitan Potatoes

Farmer's Peas and Zucchini

This delectably seasoned side dish is nice with grilled chicken.

1 tablespoon olive or vegetable oil
1 medium onion, chopped (about ¹/₂ cup)
1 tablespoon chopped fresh parsley or
*   1 teaspoon dried parsley flakes*
2 cloves garlic, finely chopped
2 medium zucchini, cut into ¹/₂-inch slices
*   (about 4 cups)*
1 package (10 ounces) frozen green peas,
*   rinsed to separate*
1 tablespoon chopped fresh parsley
2 tablespoons lemon juice
2 tablespoons dry white wine or vegetable
*   broth*
¹/₂ teaspoon salt
¹/₄ teaspoon pepper

Heat oil in 12-inch skillet over medium-high heat. Cook onion, parsley and garlic in oil 4 minutes, stirring frequently until onion is crisp-tender. Stir in remaining ingredients. Heat to boiling; reduce heat. Cook 4 to 6 minutes, stirring occasionally, until zucchini is crisp-tender. *8 servings.*

Nutrition Information Per Serving

1 serving		Percent of U.S. RDA	
Calories	50	Vitamin A	4%
Protein, g	2	Vitamin C	8%
Carbohydrate, g	8	Calcium	2%
Fat, g	2	Iron	4%
Cholesterol, mg	0		
Sodium, mg	160		

Venetian Zucchini

6 medium zucchini, cut into julienne strips
1 teaspoon salt
2 tablespoons olive or vegetable oil
2 cloves garlic, finely chopped
1 teaspoon freshly grated nutmeg
Freshly ground pepper

Spread zucchini on cutting board; sprinkle with salt. Tilt board slightly; let stand 30 minutes. Rinse zucchini; squeeze and pat dry.

Heat oil in 12-inch skillet over medium-high heat. Cook garlic in oil until soft. Stir in zucchini and nutmeg. Cook uncovered about 5 minutes, stirring frequently, until crisp-tender. Sprinkle with pepper. *6 servings.*

Nutrition Information Per Serving

1 serving		Percent of U.S. RDA	
Calories	70	Vitamin A	6%
Protein, g	2	Vitamin C	14%
Carbohydrate, g	6	Calcium	2%
Fat, g	5	Iron	4%
Cholesterol, mg	0		
Sodium, mg	360		

Zucchini with Fresh Herbs

2 medium carrots, cut into julienne strips
4 medium zucchini, cut into julienne strips
2 tablespoons margarine or butter
1 tablespoon chopped fresh or 1 teaspoon
    dried sage leaves
1 teaspoon chopped fresh or $1/4$ teaspoon
    dried dill weed
$1^1/_2$ teaspoons lemon juice
$1/4$ teaspoon salt
$1/8$ teaspoon pepper

Place steamer basket in $1/2$ inch water in 2-quart saucepan (water should not touch bottom of basket). Place carrots in basket. Cover tightly and heat to boiling; reduce heat. Steam carrots 3 minutes; add zucchini. Cover and steam 4 to 6 minutes or until carrots and zucchini are crisp-tender.

Melt margarine in 12-inch skillet over medium heat. Stir in carrots, zucchini and remaining ingredients. Cook uncovered 2 to 3 minutes, stirring gently, until hot. *4 servings.*

Nutrition Information Per Serving

1 serving		Percent of U.S. RDA	
Calories	95	Vitamin A	66%
Protein, g	3	Vitamin C	18%
Carbohydrate, g	10	Calcium	4%
Fat, g	6	Iron	6%
Cholesterol, mg	15		
Sodium, mg	190		

Spinach Milan-style

The addition of pine nuts and nutmeg turns spinach from simple to sensational!

2 pounds fresh spinach
2 tablespoons water
2 tablespoons margarine or butter
2 cloves garlic, finely chopped
$1/4$ cup pine nuts
$1/2$ teaspoon salt
$1/2$ teaspoon freshly grated nutmeg
$1/4$ teaspoon pepper

Place spinach and water in 3-quart saucepan; heat to boiling. Reduce heat; cover and cook spinach about 10 minutes or until wilted; drain well. Melt margarine in 10-inch skillet over medium-high heat. Cook garlic in margarine, stirring frequently, until tender. Stir in spinach and remaining ingredients. Cook uncovered over medium heat, stirring frequently, until hot. *4 servings.*

Nutrition Information Per Serving

1 serving		Percent of U.S. RDA	
Calories	130	Vitamin A	100%
Protein, g	5	Vitamin C	38%
Carbohydrate, g	8	Calcium	16%
Fat, g	11	Iron	26%
Cholesterol, mg	15		
Sodium, mg	440		

Baked Fennel

For the best flavor and texture, choose clean, crisp, blemish-free fennel bulbs.

4 cups water
4 large bulbs fennel, peeled and thinly
  sliced
1 large cucumber
2 tablespoons olive or vegetable oil
3 medium tomatoes, chopped (about
  2¹/₄ cups)
1 tablespoon chopped fresh basil leaves or
  ¹/₂ teaspoon dried basil leaves
1 cup seasoned dry bread crumbs
¹/₄ cup diced fully cooked smoked ham or
  prosciutto (about 2 ounces)
1 cup shredded mozzarella cheese
  (4 ounces)
1 tablespoon capers
1 tablespoon margarine or butter, softened

Heat water to boiling in 2-quart saucepan; add fennel. Boil uncovered about 7 minutes or until tender; drain.

Cut cucumber lengthwise into fourths; cut fourths crosswise into ¹/₂-inch slices. Heat oil in 10-inch skillet over medium-high heat. Cook cucumber, tomatoes and basil in oil about 5 minutes, stirring occasionally, until tomatoes soften slightly.

Heat oven to 375°. Grease rectangular baking dish, 13×9×2 inches; sprinkle with ¹/₄ cup of the bread crumbs. Layer half each of the fennel, ham, tomato mixture, cheese and remaining bread crumbs in dish; repeat. Sprinkle with capers; dot with margarine. Bake uncovered about 20 minutes or until hot and bread crumbs are golden brown. *4 servings.*

Nutrition Information Per Serving

1 serving		Percent of U.S. RDA	
Calories	370	Vitamin A	20%
Protein, g	17	Vitamin C	44%
Carbohydrate, g	45	Calcium	36%
Fat, g	17	Iron	14%
Cholesterol, mg	30		
Sodium, mg	630		

Olives

Olives with pits are almost always served in Italy, a custom that comes down to us from ancient Roman times. Pickled olives have been served as a snack or after a meal for thousands of years, and should never be confused with canned black olives. Italians linger over their olives, savoring the last taste of the olive on the pit for as long as possible before they have to relinquish the tasty kernel.

Baked Fennel

Brussels Sprouts with Prosciutto

1 pound fresh Brussels sprouts
2 tablespoons margarine or butter
¹/₂ teaspoon chicken bouillon granules
1 small onion, thinly sliced
*¹/₄ cup chopped prosciutto or fully cooked
    Virginia ham (about 2 ounces)*
*2 tablespoons freshly grated Parmesan
    cheese*

Place Brussels sprouts in 3-quart saucepan; add enough water to cover. Heat to boiling; reduce heat. Cover and simmer about 10 minutes or until stems are tender; drain.

Heat margarine and bouillon granules in 10-inch skillet over medium-high heat until margarine is melted. Cook onion in margarine 5 to 7 minutes, stirring occasionally, until tender. Stir in Brussels sprouts and prosciutto; reduce heat. Cover and cook about 2 minutes or until hot. Sprinkle with cheese. *4 servings.*

Nutrition Information Per Serving

1 serving		Percent of U.S. RDA	
Calories	120	Vitamin A	10%
Protein, g	7	Vitamin C	38%
Carbohydrate, g	10	Calcium	6%
Fat, g	8	Iron	4%
Cholesterol, mg	25		
Sodium, mg	350		

Cauliflower Gratin

*2 medium heads cauliflower (about
    2 pounds each), separated into 1-inch
    flowerets*
2 tablespoons margarine or butter
1 small onion, sliced
*¹/₂ cup diced fully cooked smoked ham or
    prosciutto (about 4 ounces)*
1 cup milk
¹/₂ cup whipping (heavy) cream
¹/₂ teaspoon salt
¹/₂ teaspoon white pepper
*¹/₂ cup shredded Fontina or Swiss cheese
    (2 ounces)*
¹/₂ cup freshly grated Parmesan cheese
¹/₂ teaspoon freshly grated nutmeg

Place cauliflower in 4-quart saucepan; add enough water to cover. Heat to boiling. Cover and boil 10 minutes; drain.

Heat oven to 375°. Melt margarine in 3-quart saucepan over low heat. Cook onion and ham in margarine about 10 minutes, stirring occasionally, until onion is tender. Stir in milk and whipping cream. Heat to boiling; reduce heat. Simmer uncovered 10 minutes, stirring occasionally. Stir in cauliflowerets.

Pour into ungreased 3-quart casserole. Sprinkle with remaining ingredients. Bake uncovered about 20 minutes or until hot and bubbly. *8 servings.*

Nutrition Information Per Serving

1 serving		Percent of U.S. RDA	
Calories	210	Vitamin A	10%
Protein, g	11	Vitamin C	58%
Carbohydrate, g	11	Calcium	20%
Fat, g	15	Iron	6%
Cholesterol, mg	50		
Sodium, mg	520		

Pesto Pasta Salad

Rotini pasta is also available in a tricolored version with white, green and red pasta.

3¹/₂ cups uncooked rotini pasta (about 8 ounces)
1 container (7 ounces) refrigerated pesto
¹/₂ cup sliced ripe olives
¹/₄ cup sliced pimiento-stuffed olives
1 jar (7 ounces) roasted red bell peppers, drained and cut into ¹/₂-inch strips (about ¹/₃ cup)
¹/₄ cup grated Parmesan cheese
¹/₄ teaspoon salt
¹/₄ teaspoon pepper
¹/₂ cup chopped walnuts, toasted

Cook pasta as directed on package. Rinse with cold water; drain. Gently toss pasta and pesto in large bowl. Stir in remaining ingredients except walnuts. Cover and refrigerate 1 to 2 hours to blend flavors. Just before serving, sprinkle with walnuts. *6 servings.*

Nutrition Information Per Serving

1 serving		Percent of U.S. RDA	
Calories	615	Vitamin A	14%
Protein, g	16	Vitamin C	84%
Carbohydrate, g	52	Calcium	26%
Fat, g	40	Iron	24%
Cholesterol, mg	10		
Sodium, mg	900		

Tortellini Salad

1 package (9 ounces) refrigerated or dried cheese-filled tortellini
1 package (9 ounces) refrigerated or dried cheese-filled spinach tortellini
²/₃ cup nonfat Italian dressing
2 tablespoons chopped fresh basil leaves
1 tablespoon freshly grated Parmesan cheese
2 tablespoons capers
¹/₈ teaspoon pepper
2 medium carrots, sliced (about 1 cup)
2 green onions, chopped

Cook tortellini as directed on package; drain. Rinse with cold water; drain. Place tortellini and remaining ingredients in large glass or plastic bowl; toss to coat tortellini with dressing. Cover and refrigerate about 2 hours or until chilled. Toss before serving. *6 servings.*

Nutrition Information Per Serving

1 serving		Percent of U.S. RDA	
Calories	200	Vitamin A	56%
Protein, g	13	Vitamin C	*
Carbohydrate, g	23	Calcium	8%
Fat, g	6	Iron	10%
Cholesterol, mg	80		
Sodium, mg	410		

Marinated Rotini Salad

To make preparing this salad even faster, try using pre-shredded cheese.

1 package (16 ounces) rotini pasta
¹/₂ cup shredded mozzarella cheese
*   (2 ounces)*
¹/₂ cup shredded Cheddar cheese
*   (2 ounces)*
¹/₄ cup freshly grated Parmesan cheese
¹/₄ cup sliced pitted imported Kalamata or
*   sliced ripe olives*
¹/₄ cup sliced pimiento-stuffed green olives
¹/₄ pound salami, cut into ¹/₄-inch pieces
¹/₂ cup chopped pepperoni (about
*   3 ounces)*
1 small red onion, chopped (about ¹/₄ cup)
³/₄ cup reduced-fat creamy Italian dressing

Cook pasta as directed on package; drain. Rinse with cold water; drain. Mix all ingredients in large glass or plastic bowl. Cover and refrigerate about 2 hours to blend flavors. Toss before serving. *8 servings.*

Nutrition Information Per Serving

1 serving		Percent of U.S. RDA	
Calories	615	Vitamin A	2%
Protein, g	24	Vitamin C	*
Carbohydrate, g	92	Calcium	16%
Fat, g	17	Iron	28%
Cholesterol, mg	35		
Sodium, mg	1260		

Bean and Tuna Salad

2 cans (15 to 16 ounces each) great
*   northern or cannellini beans, rinsed*
*   and drained*
1 medium Spanish, Bermuda or red
*   onion, thinly sliced*
¹/₃ cup olive or vegetable oil
3 tablespoons red wine vinegar
¹/₂ teaspoon salt
¹/₈ teaspoon pepper
1 can (6¹/₈ ounces) tuna in water, drained
Chopped fresh parsley

Place beans and onion in shallow glass or plastic dish. Shake oil, vinegar, salt and pepper in tightly covered container; pour over beans and onion. Cover and refrigerate at least 1 hour, stirring occasionally.

Transfer bean mixture to serving platter with slotted spoon. Break tuna into chunks; arrange on bean mixture. Sprinkle with parsley. *6 servings.*

Nutrition Information Per Serving

1 serving		Percent of U.S. RDA	
Calories	325	Vitamin A	*
Protein, g	22	Vitamin C	2%
Carbohydrate, g	38	Calcium	14%
Fat, g	13	Iron	34%
Cholesterol, mg	5		
Sodium, mg	620		

Opposite: Oil and Vinegar: (See feature on following pages) (1) and (7), Balsamic Vinegar (Modena), (2) Regular Olive Oil, (3) Red Wine Vinegar, (4) Rosemary Vinegar, (5) Extra Virgin Olive Oil, (6) Extra Light Olive Oil

Olive Oil and Vinegar

All About Olive Oil

From light to lusty, the many types of olive oil are similar to the selection found in fine wines. Olive oil ranges in flavor from delicate to rich and fruity, and in color from golden to green-gold to bright green. Personal preference and how the oil will be used determine which type of olive oil is best to buy. Because the color, price and country of origin don't necessarily reflect taste or quality, you may want to taste different brands to determine your favorite.

The increasing popularity of olive oil comes from the fact that it complements the flavors of many foods; it is becoming widely available in its various forms; and it has some positive nutritional attributes. Olive oil is a monounsaturated fat and preliminary research indicates that monounsaturated fats such as olive and peanut oils may help lower blood cholesterol. But regardless of what experts tell us about olive oil, it's still 100 percent fat, which means that it still supplies the same amount of fat and calories as butter or margarine or other oils, but the chemical properties of the oil itself are different.

Selecting Olive Oil

Olive oils are categorized according to their acidity level and the process used to make them. The best and most expensive olive oils are cold-pressed, a processing method that uses no heat or chemicals.

Extra Virgin Olive Oil: Extracted from perfectly ripe, undamaged olives by the cold-press method, which uses no heat or chemicals, this oil has the lowest acidity level of all olive oils (no more than 1 percent) and is the most expensive. Extra virgin olive oil has a more intense, fruity flavor and aroma than other grades of oil. It is recognized by its green-gold or bright green color.

Extra virgin olive oil is excellent in salad dressings for fresh, crisp greens or as an accompaniment to raw or cooked vegetables. And for true Italian taste, try dipping crusty Italian bread first into olive oil and then into a freshly shredded mound of Italy's premier Parmesan cheese, Parmigiano-Reggiano. You'll understand why Italians generally do not use butter on their bread.

Virgin Olive Oil: Extracted from olives that may be less ripe and more blemished than those of extra virgin oil, it has a low acidity level (no more than 3.3 percent) and is moderately priced. This oil has slightly less flavor and color than extra virgin olive oil.

Virgin olive oil is excellent for skillet-frying because it doesn't smoke or change flavor due to heat as extra virgin oil does. It is also good as a condiment for cooked vegetables and meats.

Pure Olive Oil: This oil is extracted from leftover olive pulp after the pressing of extra virgin oils. Heat and chemical solvents are used to aid extraction. Pure olive oil has a higher acidity level than the other oils. This oil is mild in flavor and golden in color.

Pure olive oil is a good choice for cooking and skillet-frying as it doesn't smoke easily or change flavor due to heat. This oil is also the best choice when just a hint of olive oil flavor is desired.

Light or Extra Light Oil: The term "light" refers to the flavor and color of this oil. It has the same amount of calories and fat as all olive oil. These light oils have been highly filtered resulting in a light-colored oil that tastes like vegetable oil. This olive oil can be used for high temperature frying and in baking.

Storing Olive Oil

Because oil can become rancid, proper storage is important to prolong shelf-life. Olive oil should be stored tightly covered in a dark, cool location for up to one year. It can also be refrigerated, which does not harm it, but the flavor diminishes slightly. Refrigeration also causes olive oil to become cloudy and thick, but when brought to room temperature, it becomes clear and pourable.

All About Vinegar

The word vinegar or *vin aigre* is a French term meaning "sour wine." Vinegar has been used for centuries, both for medicinal and culinary purposes.

Vinegar is made by a fermentation process that converts liquids such as wine, cider and beer into a solution of acetic acid. Acetic acid provides the characteristic, sharp flavor of vinegar.

Many countries produce vinegars, giving us a glimpse of the primary crops grown in the region. Wine-producing countries such as France, Italy and Spain manufacture varieties of *wine vinegars*.

America, known for apple pie, produces *cider vinegar*, made from apple cider. Britain, known for beer production, provides us with *malt vinegar*, which is derived from the common grain of barley. Asian nations produce rice wine vinegar using common white rice.

(continued on following page)

Selecting Vinegar

Wine Vinegar: Wine vinegar has been a familiar staple in Italian cuisine since Roman times. The Romans and Greeks had special vessels to hold vinegars, which were popular as a condiment to flavor foods. Both red and white wine are used to make vinegar. Wine vinegar often serves as the base of herb and fruit-flavored vinegars such as tarragon or raspberry. They are favored for use in salad dressings and classic sauces, such as Bernaise sauce, which uses tarragon vinegar.

Balsamic Vinegar: Balsamic vinegar dates from the eleventh century when it was a secret and was considered a luxury for the royal families of Europe. Only in the early 1900s did it become readily available for sale. Its characteristic flavor is obtained through a long process of aging and the reduction of the white Trebbiano grape juice. The juice is stored and transferred through a succession of wooden barrels. Aging takes up to 15 years, during which each barrel is closely monitored. The vinegar is usually transferred to smaller barrels every 2 years. At each interval, the vinegar is filtered and tested for sweetness and flavor development. The specific wood of the barrels contributes to refining the vinegar's flavor during the aging process. The overall result is a dark, brown-colored vinegar with a rich, mellow, smooth and slightly sweet flavor.

Balsamic vinegar can be used to add flavor to meats, seafood, poultry, sauces, salad dressings and freshly cooked vegetables. For a unique appetizer or first course, offer bite-size chunks or shavings of Parmigiano-Reggiano cheese; dip the cheese into balsamic vinegar (or sprinkle vinegar on the cheese) and serve with crusty Italian bread. Or for a simple dessert, combine fresh, sweet strawberries with a splash of balsamic vinegar.

Piquant Salad

What makes this salad piquant? Its lively, tangy flavors that combine for a marvelously refreshing salad.

8 ounces fresh green beans
1 head radicchio
1 tablespoon capers
2 medium bulbs fennel, cut into fourths
1 head Boston lettuce, torn into bite-size
 pieces
1 jar (6 ounces) marinated artichoke
 hearts, drained
1/2 cup olive or vegetable oil
2 tablespoons lemon juice
1/2 teaspoon chopped fresh mint leaves
1/2 teaspoon chopped fresh sage leaves
1/2 teaspoon chopped fresh oregano leaves
1/2 teaspoon salt
1/4 teaspoon pepper
1 clove garlic, finely chopped

Place green beans in 2-quart saucepan; add enough water to cover. Heat to boiling. Boil about 10 minutes or until crisp-tender; drain and cool.

Arrange radicchio leaves around edge of large platter. Mix beans, capers, fennel, Boston lettuce and artichoke hearts; place in center of radicchio-lined platter. Mix remaining ingredients; pour over salad. *6 servings.*

Nutrition Information Per Serving

1 serving		Percent of U.S. RDA	
Calories	225	Vitamin A	4%
Protein, g	2	Vitamin C	10%
Carbohydrate, g	11	Calcium	6%
Fat, g	19	Iron	6%
Cholesterol, mg	0		
Sodium, mg	310		

Mixed Marinated Vegetables

2 large bulbs fennel, cut into 1-inch pieces
1 pound fresh broccoli, separated into
 flowerets
4 ounces mozzarella cheese, cut into
 1/2-inch cubes
2 jars (6 ounces each) marinated
 artichoke hearts, drained
1 jar (8 ounces) marinated mushrooms,
 undrained
1 jar (10 ounces) imported Kalamata
 olives, drained and pitted*
1/2 cup olive or vegetable oil
1/2 cup red wine vinegar
2 tablespoons lemon juice

Toss all ingredients except oil, vinegar and lemon juice in shallow glass or plastic dish. Shake oil, vinegar and lemon juice in tightly covered container. Pour over vegetable mixture; toss. Cover and refrigerate about 2 hours or until chilled. Toss before serving. *8 servings.*

*One can (5.75 ounces) pitted ripe olives can be substituted for the Kalamata olives.

Nutrition Information Per Serving

1 serving		Percent of U.S. RDA	
Calories	305	Vitamin A	10%
Protein, g	8	Vitamin C	38%
Carbohydrate, g	16	Calcium	20%
Fat, g	23	Iron	14%
Cholesterol, mg	10		
Sodium, mg	700		

Antipasto Pasta Salad

1 package (16 ounces) farfalle (bow-tie) pasta
¹/₄ pound salami, diced (about ³/₄ cup)
1 small green bell pepper, cut into 1¹/₂-inch strips
1 jar (7 ounces) roasted red bell peppers, drained and cut into ¹/₄-inch strips (about ¹/₃ cup)
1 can (6 ounces) pitted large ripe black olives, drained
¹/₂ cup chopped drained pepperoncini peppers
¹/₂ cup freshly shredded Parmesan cheese
¹/₂ cup Italian dressing
2 tablespoons chopped sun-dried tomatoes in oil, drained

Cook pasta as directed on package; drain. Rinse with cold water; drain. Place pasta and remaining ingredients in large bowl; toss gently. *8 servings.*

Nutrition Information Per Serving

1 serving		Percent of U.S. RDA	
Calories	595	Vitamin A	16%
Protein, g	23	Vitamin C	100%
Carbohydrate, g	66	Calcium	16%
Fat, g	28	Iron	24%
Cholesterol, mg	35		
Sodium, mg	1470		

Italian Tomato and Bread Salad

This surprisingly different salad is sure to be a hit! It goes well with grilled meat or sausages.

4 cups 1-inch pieces day-old Italian or French bread
2 medium tomatoes, cut into bite-size pieces
2 cloves garlic, finely chopped
1 medium green bell pepper, cut into bite-size pieces
¹/₃ cup chopped fresh basil leaves
2 tablespoons chopped fresh parsley
¹/₃ cup olive or vegetable oil
2 tablespoons red wine vinegar
¹/₂ teaspoon salt
¹/₈ teaspoon pepper

Mix bread, tomatoes, garlic, bell pepper, basil and parsley in shallow glass or plastic dish. Shake remaining ingredients in tightly covered container. Pour over bread mixture; toss. Cover and refrigerate at least 1 hour. *6 servings.*

Nutrition Information Per Serving

1 serving		Percent of U.S. RDA	
Calories	165	Vitamin A	6%
Protein, g	2	Vitamin C	18%
Carbohydrate, g	13	Calcium	2%
Fat, g	12	Iron	6%
Cholesterol, mg	0		
Sodium, mg	280		

Antipasto Pasta Salad

Artichoke Summer Salad

*2 packages (9 ounces each) frozen
   artichoke hearts*
1/3 cup olive or vegetable oil
2 tablespoons balsamic vinegar
*2 teaspoons anchovy paste or finely
   chopped flat fillets of anchovy in oil*
3/4 teaspoon fennel seed, crushed
1/4 teaspoon salt
1/4 teaspoon pepper
8 cups bite-size pieces romaine
1/4 cup chopped fresh parsley
1 tablespoon capers

Cook artichoke hearts as directed on package;
drain and cool. Shake oil, vinegar, anchovy
paste, fennel seed, salt and pepper in tightly covered container. Place artichoke hearts and
romaine in large bowl. Add dressing; toss.
Sprinkle with parsley and capers. *6 servings.*

Nutrition Information Per Serving

1 serving		Percent of U.S. RDA	
Calories	160	Vitamin A	12%
Protein, g	4	Vitamin C	18%
Carbohydrate, g	12	Calcium	6%
Fat, g	12	Iron	10%
Cholesterol, mg	0		
Sodium, mg	240		

Artichoke and Bean Salad

*1 pound fresh green beans, cut into 1-inch
   pieces (about 3 cups)*
*1 can (14 ounces) quartered artichoke
   hearts, drained*
1/2 cup Pesto (page 86) or purchased pesto
*1 tablespoon freshly shredded Parmesan
   cheese*

Place green beans in 1 inch water. Heat to boiling; reduce heat. Boil uncovered 5 minutes.
Cover and boil 5 to 10 minutes longer or until
crisp-tender; drain. Stir in remaining ingredients; heat through. Serve warm or cold. *8 servings.*

Nutrition Information Per Serving

1 serving		Percent of U.S. RDA	
Calories	120	Vitamin A	4%
Protein, g	3	Vitamin C	6%
Carbohydrate, g	7	Calcium	10%
Fat, g	10	Iron	6%
Cholesterol, mg	5		
Sodium, mg	100		

Garlic and Romaine Salad

1 large bunch romaine, torn into bite-size
pieces (about 10 cups)
1 small red onion, sliced and separated
into rings
1 jar (6 ounces) marinated artichoke
hearts, undrained
1 cup pitted jumbo ripe black olives
¹/₄ cup lemon juice
2 tablespoons olive or vegetable oil
¹/₄ teaspoon salt
¹/₄ teaspoon pepper
2 cloves garlic, finely chopped
¹/₂ cup seasoned croutons
¹/₃ cup freshly shredded Parmesan cheese

Place romaine, onion, artichoke hearts and
olives in large glass or plastic bowl. Shake
lemon juice, oil, salt, pepper and garlic in tightly
covered container. Pour over romaine mixture;
toss. Sprinkle with croutons and cheese. Serve
immediately. *8 to 10 servings.*

Nutrition Information Per Serving

1 serving		Percent of U.S. RDA	
Calories	110	Vitamin A	18%
Protein, g	4	Vitamin C	16%
Carbohydrate, g	8	Calcium	10%
Fat, g	8	Iron	10%
Cholesterol, mg	5		
Sodium, mg	400		

Quick Pasta Salads

With a little imagination, leftover or
freshly cooked pasta can become cre-
ative new meals. Some might even
become family favorites! Combine
cooked, chilled pasta with the following; serve immediately or cover and
refrigerate until serving time.

- Marinated vegetables or antipasto
  mix from the deli; sprinkle with
  grated Parmesan cheese
- Dill dip from the deli and flaked
  canned salmon or tuna; sprinkle
  with chopped green onions or
  chives
- Creamy peppercorn salad dressing,
  sliced deli roast beef and precut
  vegetables from the produce section
  or salad bar
- Honey-mustard salad dressing,
  diced ham, preshredded Cheddar
  cheese and thawed frozen sugar-
  snap peas
- Southwestern ranch-style salad
  dressing, diced smoked cooked
  turkey breast, chopped red bell pepper and tomato

Warm Tomato and Olive Salad

This recipe does double duty—it's also great as an appetizer, served with chewy, fresh bread.

*1 jar (10 ounces) imported Kalamata
    olives, drained and pitted**
*1 jar (10 ounces) green olives, drained
    and pitted*
2 tablespoons olive or vegetable oil
2 tablespoons chopped fresh parsley
2 cloves garlic, finely chopped
8 small tomatoes, cut into fourths
¹/₂ teaspoon salt
¹/₄ teaspoon pepper

Cover olives with cold water. Let stand 30 minutes; drain and pat dry.

Heat oil in 10-inch skillet over medium-high heat. Cook parsley and garlic in oil, stirring frequently, until garlic is soft. Reduce heat to medium; stir in olives. Cook uncovered 3 minutes, stirring frequently. Stir in tomatoes, salt and pepper. Cook about 2 minutes, stirring gently, until tomatoes are warm. *6 servings.*

*One can (5.75 ounces) pitted ripe olives can be substituted for the Kalamata olives.

Nutrition Information Per Serving

1 serving		Percent of U.S. RDA	
Calories	165	Vitamin A	14%
Protein, g	2	Vitamin C	28%
Carbohydrate, g	11	Calcium	6%
Fat, g	14	Iron	16%
Cholesterol, mg	0		
Sodium, mg	1500		

Warm Tomato and Olive Salad

Caesar Salad

We adapted this classic salad so that it keeps all its great taste, without using any raw egg!

1 clove garlic, cut in half
8 flat fillets of anchovy in oil
¹/₃ cup olive or vegetable oil
3 tablespoons lemon juice
1 teaspoon Worcestershire sauce
¹/₄ teaspoon salt
¹/₄ teaspoon ground mustard
Freshly ground pepper
*1 large bunch romaine, torn into bite-size
    pieces (about 10 cups)*
1 cup garlic-flavored croutons
¹/₃ cup grated Parmesan cheese

Rub large wooden salad bowl with cut clove of garlic. Allow a few small pieces of garlic to remain in bowl if desired. Mix anchovies, oil, lemon juice, Worcestershire sauce, salt, mustard and pepper in bowl. Add romaine; toss until coated. Sprinkle with croutons and cheese; toss. *6 servings.*

Nutrition Information Per Serving

1 serving		Percent of U.S. RDA	
Calories	180	Vitamin A	14%
Protein, g	5	Vitamin C	10%
Carbohydrate, g	6	Calcium	10%
Fat, g	15	Iron	6%
Cholesterol, mg	10		
Sodium, mg	460		

7

Desserts

Anise Biscotti (page 153); Mocha Biscotti (page 152)

Mocha Biscotti

Biscotti means "twice baked" and that is the technique that gives these cookies their crisp texture. This delightful recipe combines three favorite flavors—coffee, chocolate and toasted almond.

*2 tablespoons instant espresso or coffee
        crystals*
2 teaspoons hot water
1 cup sugar
*¹/₂ cup (1 stick) margarine or butter,
        softened*
1 teaspoon vanilla
2 eggs
3¹/₂ cups all-purpose flour
*¹/₂ ounces semisweet chocolate, grated
        (about ¹/₂ cup)*
*¹/₄ cup slivered almonds, toasted and
        chopped*
1 teaspoon baking powder
¹/₂ teaspoon salt

Heat oven to 350°. Dissolve coffee crystals in hot water. Beat sugar, margarine, vanilla, eggs and coffee in large bowl. Stir in remaining ingredients.

On ungreased cookie sheet, shape half of dough at a time into rectangle, 10 × 3 inches, rounding edges slightly. Bake about 30 minutes or until center is firm to the touch. Cool on cookie sheet 15 minutes.

Cut crosswise into ¹/₂-inch slices. Place slices, cut sides down, on cookie sheet. Bake about 15 minutes, turning once, until crisp and edges are light brown. Immediately remove from cookie sheet. Cool on wire rack. *About 3¹/₂ dozen cookies.*

Chocolate-drizzled Mocha Biscotti: Heat 3 ounces semisweet chocolate or white chocolate baking bar and ¹/₂ teaspoon shortening in 1-quart saucepan over low heat, stirring occasionally, until melted and smooth. Place cooled biscotti, cut sides up, on waxed paper. Drizzle chocolate over one side of each biscotti. Let stand until chocolate is set.

Nutrition Information Per Serving

1 cookie		Percent of U.S. RDA	
Calories	85	Vitamin A	2%
Protein, g	1	Vitamin C	*
Carbohydrate, g	13	Calcium	*
Fat, g	3	Iron	2%
Cholesterol, mg	10		
Sodium, mg	65		

Anise Biscotti

If anise seed is unavailable, or if you'd like something a bit different, try the Orange Biscotti variation.

> *1 cup sugar*
> *½ cup (1 stick) margarine or butter, softened*
> *2 teaspoons anise seed, ground*
> *2 teaspoons grated lemon peel*
> *2 eggs*
> *3½ cups all-purpose flour*
> *1 teaspoon baking powder*
> *½ teaspoon salt*

Heat oven to 350°. Beat sugar, margarine, anise, lemon peel and eggs in large bowl. Stir in flour, baking powder and salt.

On ungreased cookie sheet, shape half of dough at a time into rectangle, 10 × 3 inches, rounding edges slightly. Bake about 20 minutes or until center is firm to the touch. Cool on cookie sheet 15 minutes.

Cut crosswise into ½-inch slices. Place slices, cut sides down, on cookie sheet. Bake about 15 minutes or until crisp and light brown. Immediately remove from cookie sheet. Cool on wire rack. *About 3 ½ dozen cookies.*

Orange Biscotti: Omit anise seed and lemon peel. Add 1 tablespoon grated orange peel to the margarine mixture.

Nutrition Information Per Serving

1 cookie		Percent of U.S. RDA	
Calories	85	Vitamin A	2%
Protein, g	1	Vitamin C	*
Carbohydrate, g	13	Calcium	*
Fat, g	3	Iron	2%
Cholesterol, mg	10		
Sodium, mg	65		

Amaretti

"A little bitter" is the translation of amaretti. Traditionally, Italians use half bitter almonds and half regular almonds to make these cookies. Bitter almonds are harvested before they are ripe. As bitter almonds are hard to find here, our recipe uses regular almonds, which gives the cookies a slightly different, but just as delicious, flavor.

3 cups slivered almonds, toasted
3 jumbo egg whites
1¹/₂ cups granulated sugar
1 teaspoon powdered sugar
1 teaspoon amaretto or almond extract
Granulated sugar

Heat oven to 300°. Line cookie sheet with cooking parchment paper, or grease and flour cookie sheet.

Place almonds in food processor or blender. Cover and process until finely ground but not pastelike.

Beat egg whites in medium bowl on high speed until stiff. Stir in almonds, 1¹/₂ cups granulated sugar, the powdered sugar and amaretto. Drop by rounded teaspoonfuls about 2 inches apart onto cookie sheet. Sprinkle with granulated sugar. Bake 20 to 25 minutes or until brown. Cool 5 minutes; remove from cookie sheet. Cool on wire rack. *About 4 dozen cookies.*

Nutrition Information Per Serving

1 cookie		Percent of U.S. RDA	
Calories	70	Vitamin A	*
Protein, g	1	Vitamin C	*
Carbohydrate, g	8	Calcium	2%
Fat, g	4	Iron	*
Cholesterol, mg	0		
Sodium, mg	10		

Sweet Sighs

These meringue-based cookies are light and delicate—perfect served with coffee or an ice such as Strawberry-Orange Ice (page 170).

¹/₂ cup sugar
2 egg whites
¹/₂ cup slivered almonds, toasted and coarsely crushed
2 teaspoons grated lemon peel

Heat oven to 325°. Line cookie sheet with cooking parchment paper, or grease and flour cookie sheet. Beat sugar and egg whites in small bowl on high speed until stiff. Stir in almonds and lemon peel. Drop by tablespoonfuls about 2 inches apart onto cookie sheet. Bake 20 to 25 minutes or until edges are light golden brown. Cool 5 minutes; remove from cookie sheet. Cool on wire rack. *15 cookies.*

Nutrition Information Per Serving

1 cookie		Percent of U.S. RDA	
Calories	55	Vitamin A	*
Protein, g	1	Vitamin C	*
Carbohydrate, g	8	Calcium	*
Fat, g	2	Iron	*
Cholesterol, mg	0		
Sodium, mg	10		

Pizzelles

These Italian cookies are wafer thin and lightly flavored with anise. They are cooked in a special pizzelle iron, which is available in most specialty cookware stores. If you'd like your cookies in a cylinder shape, quickly roll them into a cylinder as soon as you remove them from the pizzelle iron. Work quickly— they cool very fast!

2 cups all-purpose flour
1 cup sugar
³/₄ cup (1¹/₂ sticks) margarine or butter, melted and cooled
1 tablespoon anise extract or vanilla
2 teaspoons baking powder
4 eggs, slightly beaten

Lightly grease pizzelle iron. Heat pizzelle iron as directed by manufacturer. Mix all ingredients. Drop 1 tablespoon batter onto each design of heated pizzelle iron; close iron. Bake about 30 seconds or until golden brown. Carefully remove pizzelle from iron; cool. Repeat with remaining batter. *About 3¹/₂ dozen cookies.*

Nutrition Information Per Serving

1 cookie		Percent of U.S. RDA	
Calories	80	Vitamin A	4%
Protein, g	1	Vitamin C	*
Carbohydrate, g	10	Calcium	2%
Fat, g	4	Iron	2%
Cholesterol, mg	20		
Sodium, mg	65		

Tira Mi Su

**Literally translated, this means " lift me up."
Tira Mi Su was named for its restorative
properties—the cream, egg yolks and cheese
were thought to be excellent for those in poor
health. The addition of rum and espresso
should give a lift to those in the best of
health!**

> *6 egg yolks*
> *³/₄ cup sugar*
> *²/₃ cup milk*
> *1 pound mascarpone cheese or 2 packages
>   (8 ounces each) cream cheese,
>   softened*
> *1¹/₄ cups whipping (heavy) cream*
> *¹/₂ teaspoon vanilla*
> *¹/₄ cup cold prepared espresso or very
>   strong coffee*
> *2 tablespoons rum**
> *2 packages (3 ounces each) ladyfingers*
> *1 tablespoon cocoa*

Beat egg yolks and sugar in 2-quart saucepan on
medium speed about 30 seconds or until well
blended. Beat in milk. Heat to boiling over
medium heat, stirring constantly. Reduce heat to
low. Boil and stir 1 minute; remove from heat.
Place plastic wrap or waxed paper directly onto
milk mixture in saucepan. Refrigerate about
1 hour.

Mix milk mixture and cheese. Beat whipping
cream and vanilla in chilled medium bowl until
stiff. Mix espresso and rum.

Separate ladyfingers horizontally. Brush or drizzle 24 of the ladyfingers with espresso mixture
(do not soak). Arrange in single layer in
ungreased rectangular baking dish, 11 × 7 ×
1¹/₂ inches. Spread half the cheese mixture over
ladyfingers. Spread half the whipped cream
over cheese mixture. Repeat with remaining
ladyfingers, cheese mixture and whipped cream.
Sprinkle with cocoa. Refrigerate 4 to 6 hours or
until firm. *8 servings.*

**¹/₈ teaspoon rum extract mixed with 2 table-
spoons water can be substituted for the rum.*

Nutrition Information Per Serving

1 serving		Percent of U.S. RDA	
Calories	540	Vitamin A	38%
Protein, g	9	Vitamin C	*
Carbohydrate, g	36	Calcium	12%
Fat, g	39	Iron	8%
Cholesterol, mg	310		
Sodium, mg	250		

Cassata

Sponge Cake (page 162)*
¹/₂ cup rum**
¹/₂ cup chopped candied fruit or golden raisins
1 cup coffee ice cream, slightly softened
1 cup Neapolitan ice cream, slightly softened***
¹/₃ cup whipping (heavy) cream
1 tablespoon powdered sugar

Place loaf pan, 8¹/₂ × 4¹/₂ × 2¹/₂ inches, in freezer. Prepare Sponge Cake. Pour rum over candied fruit; let stand 1 hour. Drain fruit, reserving rum.

Cut a rectangle from one end of cake to fit loaf pan, 8¹/₂ × 4¹/₂ inches. (Wrap and freeze remaining cake for another use.) Drizzle reserved rum over cake.

Remove loaf pan from freezer. Spread coffee ice cream in pan; freeze until firm. Spread Neapolitan ice cream over ice cream in pan; freeze until firm.

Beat whipping cream and powdered sugar in chilled small bowl on high speed until stiff. Fold in candied fruit. Spread whipping cream mixture over ice cream in pan. Top with rum-soaked cake.

Cover and freeze about 8 hours or until firm. Loosen edges with knife; unmold. *6 servings.*

*Purchased pound cake can be substituted for the Sponge Cake. Wrap and freeze any remaining cake for another use.

**2 teaspoons rum extract mixed with ¹/₂ cup water can be substituted for the rum.

***Equal amounts of strawberry, vanilla and chocolate ice cream can be substituted if Neapolitan ice cream is unavailable.

Nutrition Information Per Serving

1 serving		Percent of U.S. RDA	
Calories	445	Vitamin A	16%
Protein, g	8	Vitamin C	*
Carbohydrate, g	57	Calcium	10%
Fat, g	16	Iron	8%
Cholesterol, mg	180		
Sodium, mg	290		

Cannoli

Cannoli are tubular pastry shells that have been deep-fried. They are available in the gourmet section of large supermarkets and in specialty food shops.

> *1 cup powdered sugar*
> *1 container (15 ounces) ricotta cheese*
> *$\frac{1}{2}$ cup slivered almonds, toasted*
> *$\frac{1}{3}$ cup miniature semisweet chocolate*
> *   chips*
> *1 tablespoon amaretto**
> *12 cannoli pastry shells*
> *1 tablespoon powdered sugar*
> *1 tablespoon cocoa*
> *Maraschino or fresh sweet cherries*

Gradually stir 1 cup powdered sugar into cheese in large bowl. Stir in almonds, chocolate chips and amaretto. Carefully spoon filling into pastry shells, filling from the center out. Sprinkle individual serving plates with powdered sugar and cocoa or sprinkle on cannoli. Garnish plates with cherries. *12 pastries.*

*$\frac{1}{8}$ teaspoon almond extract mixed with 1 tablespoon water can be substituted for the amaretto.

Nutrition Information Per Serving

1 pastry		Percent of U.S. RDA	
Calories	220	Vitamin A	8%
Protein, g	6	Vitamin C	*
Carbohydrate, g	24	Calcium	12%
Fat, g	11	Iron	4%
Cholesterol, mg	10		
Sodium, mg	125		

Flambéed Desserts

Some dishes are flamed only for dramatic effect, but flaming can also be an important part of the cooking process. The alcohol burns off, but the flavor of the liquor remains. Use the amount of liquor called for—too much alcohol and the flames can burn the food, leaving a charred taste. Flames should not burn longer than a minute and, as a safety precaution, a lid should always be on hand to extinguish the flames, if necessary. Normally, rum, vodka and other spirits burn themselves out in a minute, but they can flame up if the dish is placed over heat again.

Zuppa Inglese

The name of this dessert translates as "English Soup Cake," and is a variation of the classic English dessert trifle. It may have made its way to Florence by way of the employees who worked in the London offices of Florentine banking houses.

> *Sponge Cake (below)*
> *1/2 cup plus 2 tablespoons sugar*
> *2 eggs*
> *3 tablespoons all-purpose flour*
> *2 cups milk*
> *2 ounces unsweetened chocolate, grated*
> *1/2 cup rum**
> *1/2 cup cherry-flavored liqueur***

Prepare Sponge Cake. Beat sugar and eggs in 2-quart saucepan. Gradually stir in flour. Heat milk to scalding; gradually stir into sugar mixture. Cook over low heat 10 minutes, stirring constantly. Stir in chocolate. Cook 2 minutes, stirring constantly, until chocolate is melted. Cover and refrigerate until cool.

Mix rum and liqueur; sprinkle over cake. Cut cake crosswise into 4 rectangles, 9 × 3 1/4 inches. Place one cake rectangle in ungreased loaf pan, 9 × 5 × 3 inches. Spread with one-fourth of the filling. Repeat layering 3 times. Cover and refrigerate at least 2 hours. *8 servings.*

SPONGE CAKE

> *1 tablespoon plus 1 teaspoon sugar*
> *1 tablespoon all-purpose flour*
> *3 jumbo eggs*
> *1/2 cup sugar*
> *3/4 cup all-purpose flour*
> *1/2 teaspoon salt*

Heat oven to 325°. Grease rectangular pan, 13 × 9 × 2 inches. Line bottom with waxed paper; grease waxed paper. Mix 1 tablespoon plus 1 teaspoon sugar and 1 tablespoon flour. Coat pan with sugar mixture.

Beat eggs in medium bowl on high speed 5 minutes or until thickened. Gradually beat in 1/2 cup sugar. Mix 3/4 cup flour and the salt; fold into egg mixture. Pour into pan.

Bake about 20 minutes or until toothpick inserted in center comes out clean. Cool 5 minutes. Invert pan onto heatproof surface; remove waxed paper. Cool cake completely.

*1/2 teaspoon rum extract mixed with 1/2 cup water can be substituted for the rum.

**1/2 teaspoon almond extract mixed with 1/2 cup water can be substituted for the cherry-flavored liqueur.

Nutrition Information Per Serving

1 serving		Percent of U.S. RDA	
Calories	380	Vitamin A	8%
Protein, g	9	Vitamin C	*
Carbohydrate, g	50	Calcium	10%
Fat, g	9	Iron	10%
Cholesterol, mg	160		
Sodium, mg	210		

Opposite: Italian Beverages: (See feature on following pages) (1) Asti, (2) Chianti (bottle and glass to right), (3) Raspberry Soda Bottle and Glass with Spritz, (4) Galliano, (5) Latte, (6) Red Table Wine, (7)Cappuccino, (8) Sambuco, (9) Marsala, (10) Espresso, (11) Grappa (small glass and decanter)

Beverages

Coffee

Coffee or "caffe" in Italian is a name that represents not only cappuccino, espresso, latte and mocha, but also means cafe or coffee house. Since coffee was introduced in Venice in the sixteenth century, Italians have consumed and loved freshly ground, strong, black coffee. The length of time coffee beans are roasted affects its flavor and color. Italian roasted beans are dark brown in color and produce a dark, strong brew. These beans are preferred for the specialty coffees listed below although any dark roast will also be effective.

Espresso: Often mispronounced "expresso," true espresso is clean and assertive in flavor, with little aftertaste and no bitterness. Espresso is made with an espresso coffee maker, which forces steam or hot water through finely ground beans and is usually served in small, one-ounce portions. Italians drink espresso throughout the day, but it is not served with the embellishments Americans favor, such as sugar or twists of lemon peel. Instant espresso powder is available in supermarkets.

Cappuccino: Named after the color of the traditional capes of Italian monks, cappuccino is a blend of $1/3$ espresso and $2/3$ steamed milk, which is frothy. In America, the froth is often sprinkled with cinnamon, nutmeg or cocoa, and a biscotti or pirouette cookie rests on the saucer for dipping. Americans savor cappuccino after dinner, whereas Italians drink it only in the morning.

Corretto: Starting with espresso, other ingredients are added such as alcohol, cocoa, soda or syrups.

Latte: A latte is a blend of $1/3$ espresso and $2/3$ heated milk; there is no frothy cap as in cappuccino.

Sodas

Italian sodas are sparkling beverages freshly made with soda water and nonalcoholic fruit syrups poured over ice. Soda water is water that has been charged with carbon dioxide to produce effervescence and is also referred to as club soda or seltzer. A wide variety of fruit-flavored syrups are available, and the end result is a very refreshing beverage.

Alcoholic Beverages

The Italian landscape is dotted with lush grape vineyards that produce many fine wines. Italy has a drink for every occasion—wine to better enjoy food; sparkling Spumante for celebrations; Marsala and sweet wines for dessert or appetizers; Grappa and other brandies to give a sense of warmth; glowing Sambuca or Amaretto liqueurs for particular romantic or special occasions. Italy offers over 200 wine and spirit selections, but we've selected the most popular exports to highlight.

Alchermes: A strong cherry liqueur with a sweetness similar to maraschino cherries, it is used for soaking cakes and pastries.

Asti Spumante: This is a bubbly white wine similar to champagne, named for the Asti region in Piedmont. It has a sweet, fruity flavor and is generally served with dessert or reserved for holiday occasions.

Chianti: One of the best-known red Italian wines, it comes from the Chianti district near Florence. Chianti has a warm, fruity flavor that can be served with most meats and pasta.

Grappa: A brandy made from either grapes or apples. Grappa is popular in northern Italian regions. Grappa may have a wildflower seasoning added to it.

Lambrusco: A bubbly red wine that is slightly sweet and fruity. Lambrusco goes well with lightly spiced foods and is often selected for holiday occasions.

Marsala: This is an amber-colored wine from Sicily, with a flavor similar to sherry. Marsala can be sweet or dry. Dry Marsala is used for savory dishes such as Chicken Marsala (see page 95), and sweet Marsala is used for sweet dishes such as Strawberries with Marsala Sauce (see page 167).

Sambuca: Traditionally light blue-colored in Italy, this syrupy liqueur is available either clear or in a dramatic transparent black color in America. It has a sweet anise flavor and is usually served with espresso coffee beans floating on top. Sambuca is traditionally served after dinner with dessert or espresso.

Flambéed Bananas with Amaretto

When selecting alcohol for this—or any other—flaming dessert, note that those labeled 80 proof or higher ignite more quickly and burn longer.

4 bananas
2 tablespoons margarine or butter
1 tablespoon granulated sugar
1 tablespoon packed brown sugar
$1/2$ cup whipping (heavy) cream
$1/4$ teaspoon ground cinnamon
$1/4$ cup amaretto*

Peel bananas; cut in half lengthwise. Heat margarine in 10-inch skillet over medium heat until melted. Stir in sugars. Cook bananas in sugar mixture, turning once, until browned and glazed. Carefully remove bananas to heatproof serving platter.

Beat whipping cream and cinnamon in chilled bowl at medium speed until stiff. Spoon or pipe whipped cream around bananas. Heat amaretto in small, long-handled pan or metal ladle just until warm. Carefully ignite and pour flaming amaretto over bananas. Serve hot after flame dies. Serve immediately. *4 servings.*

*$1/4$ teaspoon almond extract mixed with $1/4$ cup water can be substituted for the amaretto. Heat mixture in small saucepan; pour over bananas. **Note: *Mixture will not ignite.***

Nutrition Information Per Serving

1 serving		Percent of U.S. RDA	
Calories	315	Vitamin A	14%
Protein, g	2	Vitamin C	6%
Carbohydrate, g	39	Calcium	2%
Fat, g	17	Iron	2%
Cholesterol, mg	55		
Sodium, mg	55		

Flambéed Raspberries

2 tablespoons margarine or butter
1 tablespoon sugar
3 tablespoons orange-flavored liqueur*
2 tablespoons lemon juice
2 pints fresh raspberries
¹/₄ cup rum**
¹/₄ cup brandy***
Vanilla ice cream, if desired

Heat margarine in 10-inch skillet over medium heat until melted. Sprinkle sugar over margarine. Cook, stirring constantly, until sugar is brown. Stir in liqueur and lemon juice. Heat to boiling, stirring constantly. Boil and stir 1 minute. Gently stir in raspberries. Pour rum and brandy over raspberries. Heat over high heat until hot. Carefully ignite. Spoon raspberry mixture over ice cream when flame dies. *6 servings.*

*¹/₄ teaspoon orange extract mixed with 3 tablespoons water can be substituted for the orange-flavored liqueur. **Note: Mixture will not ignite.**

¹/₄ teaspoon rum extract mixed with ¹/₄ cup water can be substituted for the rum. **Note: Mixture will not ignite.

***¹/₄ teaspoon brandy extract mixed with ¹/₄ cup water can be substituted for the brandy. **Note: Mixture will not ignite.**

Nutrition Information Per Serving

1 serving		Percent of U.S. RDA	
Calories	275	Vitamin A	14%
Protein, g	3	Vitamin C	20%
Carbohydrate, g	30	Calcium	10%
Fat, g	16	Iron	2%
Cholesterol, mg	55		
Sodium, mg	70		

Strawberries with Marsala Sauce

1 quart strawberries
2 cups sweet Marsala wine or orange juice
¹/₂ cup sugar
6 egg yolks

Remove stems from strawberries. Arrange strawberries, stem sides down, in serving dish. Pour 1 cup of the wine over strawberries.

Beat sugar and egg yolks in top of double boiler, using wire whisk, until pale yellow and slightly thickened. Pour just enough water into bottom of double boiler so that top of double boiler does not touch water. Heat water over medium heat (do not boil). Place top of double boiler over bottom. Gradually beat remaining wine into egg yolk mixture. Cook, beating constantly, until mixture thickens and coats wire whisk (do not boil). Immediately pour over strawberries and wine. *6 servings.*

Nutrition Information Per Serving

1 serving		Percent of U.S. RDA	
Calories	200	Vitamin A	8%
Protein, g	4	Vitamin C	100%
Carbohydrate, g	33	Calcium	4%
Fat, g	6	Iron	6%
Cholesterol, mg	210		
Sodium, mg	10		

Italian Fruit Salad

Asti Spumante is a sweet, sparkling white wine from northern Italy similar to champagne. Asti Spumante has more natural sugars, so it is excellent with—and in—desserts.

¹/₂ cup amaretto*
¹/₂ cup Asti Spumante or sparkling apple juice
2 tablespoons sugar
2 tablespoons lemon juice
1 pint strawberries, sliced
1 cup seedless grapes
2 medium unpeeled eating apples, cored and cut up
2 medium unpeeled pears, cored and cut up
2 medium bananas, sliced
2 kiwifruit or figs, peeled and sliced
¹/₂ cup Asti Spumante or apple juice

Mix amaretto, ¹/₂ cup Asti Spumante, the sugar and lemon juice in large serving bowl. Add remaining ingredients except ¹/₂ cup Asti Spumante; toss. Cover and refrigerate at least 1 hour.

Immediately before serving, pour ¹/₂ cup Asti Spumante over fruit; toss. Top each serving with sherbet if desired. *8 servings.*

*¹/₂ teaspoon almond extract mixed with ¹/₂ cup water can be substituted for the amaretto.

Nutrition Information Per Serving

1 serving		Percent of U.S. RDA	
Calories	240	Vitamin A	*
Protein, g	1	Vitamin C	82%
Carbohydrate, g	41	Calcium	2%
Fat, g	1	Iron	4%
Cholesterol, mg	0		
Sodium, mg	10		

Amaretto Ice Cream

¹/₂ cup amaretto*
¹/₂ cup golden raisins
³/₄ cup sugar
1 cup whole milk
1 egg
6 Amaretti (page 154) or 12 purchased Amaretti cookies, crushed (about ¹/₂ cup)
1 cup whipping (heavy) cream
¹/₄ teaspoon salt

Pour amaretto over raisins; let stand at least 8 hours. Drain, reserving 2 tablespoons amaretto.

Mix sugar, milk and egg in 2-quart saucepan. Cook over medium heat, stirring constantly, 5 or 6 minutes or until mixture reaches 165°. Remove from heat. Cover and refrigerate about 1¹/₂ hours or until cool.

Stir cookies into milk mixture. Beat whipping cream in chilled medium bowl until stiff. Fold milk mixture into whipped cream. Fold in reserved amaretto, the raisins and salt. Freeze in ice-cream maker as directed by manufacturer. *About 1 quart ice cream (8 servings).*

*¹/₂ teaspoon almond extract mixed with ¹/₂ cup water can be substituted for the amaretto.

Nutrition Information Per Serving

1 serving		Percent of U.S. RDA	
Calories	315	Vitamin A	10%
Protein, g	2	Vitamin C	*
Carbohydrate, g	40	Calcium	4%
Fat, g	16	Iron	4%
Cholesterol, mg	80		
Sodium, mg	130		

Italian Fruit Salad

Lemon Ice

For a beautiful dessert, serve this ice in hollowed-out fresh lemon halves. Cut off a portion of the lemon bottom so that it sits flat on the plate; then garnish with mint leaves.

2 cups water
1 cup sugar
1 tablespoon grated lemon peel
1 cup lemon juice

Heat water and sugar to boiling in 2-quart saucepan; reduce heat. Simmer uncovered 5 minutes; remove from heat. Stir in lemon peel and lemon juice. Cool to room temperature. Pour into loaf pan, 9 × 5 × 3 inches. Freeze 3 to 4 hours, stirring every 30 minutes.

Serve in chilled dessert dishes. (If ice is not to be served immediately, cut into ¹/₂-inch chunks; place in bowl. Cover and freeze until serving time.) *8 servings.*

Nutrition Information Per Serving

1 serving		Percent of U.S. RDA	
Calories	110	Vitamin A	*
Protein, g	0	Vitamin C	4%
Carbohydrate, g	27	Calcium	*
Fat, g	0	Iron	*
Cholesterol, mg	0		
Sodium, mg	10		

Strawberry-Orange Ice

Italians have been in love with ices and ice cream for hundreds of years. In Florence during the Renaissance, special icehouses were built so that cooks would always have access to the ice needed to make their delicious confections.

2 cups water
¹/₃ cup sugar
¹/₂ cup freshly squeezed orange juice
12 very ripe strawberries, mashed well
(about ¹/₂ cup)
1 teaspoon vanilla

Heat water to boiling in 2-quart saucepan. Stir in remaining ingredients. Boil 3 minutes, stirring constantly. Cool 10 minutes. Freeze in ice-cream maker as directed by manufacturer. Allow to stand at room temperature at least 30 minutes before serving. *1 quart ice.*

Nutrition Information Per Serving

1 serving (¹/₄ cup)		Percent of U.S. RDA	
Calories	25	Vitamin A	*
Protein, g	0	Vitamin C	6%
Carbohydrate, g	6	Calcium	*
Fat, g	0	Iron	*
Cholesterol, mg	0		
Sodium, mg	0		

Strawberry-Orange Ice

METRIC CONVERSION GUIDE

U.S. UNITS	CANADIAN METRIC	AUSTRALIAN METRIC
Volume		
1/4 teaspoon	1 mL	1 ml
1/2 teaspoon	2 mL	2 ml
1 teaspoon	5 mL	5 ml
1 tablespoon	15 mL	20 ml
1/4 cup	50 mL	60 ml
1/3 cup	75 mL	80 ml
1/2 cup	125 mL	125 ml
2/3 cup	150 mL	170 ml
3/4 cup	175 mL	190 ml
1 cup	250 mL	250 ml
1 quart	1 liter	1 liter
1 1/2 quarts	1.5 liter	1.5 liter
2 quarts	2 liters	2 liters
2 1/2 quarts	2.5 liters	2.5 liters
3 quarts	3 liters	3 liters
4 quarts	4 liters	4 liters
Weight		
1 ounce	30 grams	30 grams
2 ounces	55 grams	60 grams
3 ounces	85 grams	90 grams
4 ounces (1/4 pound)	115 grams	125 grams
8 ounces (1/2 pound)	225 grams	225 grams
16 ounces (1 pound)	455 grams	500 grams
1 pound	455 grams	1/2 kilogram

Measurements		Temperatures	
Inches	Centimeters	Fahrenheit	Celsius
1	2.5	32°	0°
2	5.0	212°	100°
3	7.5	250°	120°
4	10.0	275°	140°
5	12.5	300°	150°
6	15.0	325°	160°
7	17.5	350°	180°
8	20.5	375°	190°
9	23.0	400°	200°
10	25.5	425°	220°
11	28.0	450°	230°
12	30.5	475°	240°
13	33.0	500°	260°
14	35.5		
15	38.0		

NOTE
The recipes in this cookbook have not been developed or tested using metric measures. When converting recipes to metric, some variations in quality may be noted.

Index

Numbers in *italics* refer to illustrations.